SECRET
BOSTON

SECRET
BOSTON

The Unique Guidebook to Boston's Hidden Sites, Sounds, & Tastes

Laura Purdom

WITH PHOTOGRAPHS BY
Linda Rutenberg

ECW PRESS

The publication of *Secret Boston* has been generously supported by the Canada Council, the Ontario Arts Council, and the Government of Canada through the Book Publishing Industry Development Program. **Canada**

NATIONAL LIBRARY OF CANADA CATALOGUING IN PUBLICATION DATA

Purdom, Laura, 1960-
Secret Boston: the unique guidebook to Boston's hidden sites,
sounds, & tastes
Includes index.
ISBN 1-55022-488-3
1. Boston (Mass.) – Guidebooks. I. Title.
F73.18.P87 2002   917.44'610444   C2001-903591-8

Original series design: Paul Davies, ECW Type and Art, Oakville, Ontario.
Series editor: Laura Byrne Paquet.
Typesetting: Martel *en-tête*.
Imaging and cover: Guylaine Régimbald – SOLO DESIGN.
Printed by Transcontinental.

Distributed in Canada by General Distribution Services,
325 Humber College Boulevard, Etobicoke, Ontario M9W 7C3.

Distributed in the United States by Independent Publishers Group,
814 North Franklin Street, Chicago, Illinois 60610.

Published by ECW PRESS
2120 Queen Street East, Suite 200, Toronto, Ontario M4E 1E2.

ecwpress.com

PRINTED AND BOUND IN CANADA

TABLE OF CONTENTS

SECRET . . .

INTRODUCTION

I know your kind. You see a swarm of tourists heading one way, and you head the other. You'd rather look at the edgy and unknown than another Monet retrospective. You prefer hole-in-the-wall cafés to flavor-of-the-month restaurants. And you'd rather appreciate local talent — or join in a jam — than pay big bucks for Broadway.

This book is for you: the tourist errant. You're the urban explorer who tries exotic foods, trots down alleys, chats with the locals. You've heard about the Freedom Trail, Boston's two-mile Revolutionary march. Maybe you've even trekked it. But now you've pried your eyes from that painted red line and you're ready to start your own revolution.

This book exists, as well, for Bostonians who want a cool little guide to their city, one that turns up surprises in old familiar places and leads the way to the new and unknown. While *Secret Boston* takes a look at the very new — from new hotels to theaters to arts spaces — it also offers signposts to and around the places and activities that we hope will never change. Revere Beach's flesh parade. An espresso at Café Pamplona. Five-for-a-dollar plums at Haymarket. Fenway's Green Monster. The far reaches of the Emerald Necklace.

Whether it's your first visit to Boston or you've lived here since the last Ice Age, *Secret Boston* invites you to do some urban bushwhacking. Meet Phineas Gage, the "crowbar man," whose medical trauma changed the way we think about the brain. Cruise the Cambridge Canal with your *amore* in a Venetian gondola. Stomp your feet to old-time bluegrass at a weekly Cambridge jam session. Celebrate Bastille Day, pin a dollar on St. Anthony, and cheer on the Hong Kong Dragonboat racers. Imagine the roar of the crowd at the site of baseball's first World Series, when Cy Young led the Boston Pilgrims to victory against the Pittsburgh Pirates. Stuff yourself with moon cakes in a Chinatown bakery. Tour a working 19th-century frame mill. Listen to some of the best Irish music this side of Limerick. Stay the night on a yacht. View the art of Dr. Jack Kevorkian.

HOW TO USE
SECRET BOSTON

This book is arranged alphabetically. You can flip to your favorite obsession, be it "Architecture" or "Barbecue," or develop a new fixation by browsing such categories as "Candlepins," "'Doctor Death,'" "Experienced Apparel," "Fruits and Veggies," and so on, all the way to "Yoga."

As if that brilliant little scheme weren't enough, at the back of this book you'll find a subject index that groups sites and events by interest (such as festivals, kids' stuff, and restaurants). Also, cross-references appear from time to time within the text to alert you to related subjects.

Where appropriate, I've noted hours and adult admission fees. For most places, it is safe to assume that there are reduced fees for children (usually about half the adult fee), seniors, and (sometimes) students. In any case, it's smart to call in advance because hours and fees will change. And, sadly, sometimes places disappear, especially the sort of offbeat attractions I traffic in here. So, do use the phone numbers I went to so much trouble to type. Note that for calls anywhere within Greater Boston (including Cambridge), you must *dial 10 digits* — that is, the area code along with the phone number. While most of this book stays within the homey 617 area code, I couldn't resist putting in a few morsels further afield. If you're calling between the 617 area and any other Greater Boston area, you must prefix the 10-digit number with "1." Addresses are in Boston, except where otherwise noted.

OTHER RESOURCES

A number of publications keep Bostonians abreast of events and entertainment. The *Improper Bostonian* has comprehensive listings of what's going on around town, including some offbeat stuff. Find the new issue every couple of weeks on street corners everywhere. The *Boston Phoenix* comes out every week with its thick-as-a-bible "Eight Days a Week" entertainment section. You have to pay for the *Boston Globe*, which publishes the weekly "Calendar" pullout each Thursday with restaurant reviews and regional happenings from harpsichord concerts to Israeli folk dancing to poetry slams. *Boston* magazine features up-market commentary and restaurant reviews with an "editor's pick" section previewing a few of the coming month's entertainment events. See "Secret Theater," "Secret GLBT," and "Secret Rock" for alternative news sources.

The **Greater Boston Convention and Visitors Bureau** (888-733-2678 or 617-536-4100, www.bostonusa.com) offers information as well as assistance with restaurant and hotel reservations. For walk-in service there is the Boston Common Visitor Information Center (147 Tremont Street, near Park Street station), open Monday to Saturday (8:30 AM to 5 PM), and Sundays (9 AM to 5 PM), where you can talk with one of the staff people and browse hundreds of brochures. In the Back Bay, you'll find another GBC&VB outpost at the Prudential

Center Visitor Information Center. Open weekdays (8:30 AM to 6 PM) and weekends (10 AM to 6 PM). Across the river, the **Cambridge Visitor Information Booth** (800-862-5678) is located in a kiosk in the middle of Harvard Square. Open Monday to Saturday. The **State Tourism Office** (800-227-6277, www.mass-vacation.com) is another useful resource.

For information on subways, trains, and city buses, contact the MBTA (617-222-3200, www.mbta.com), or Metropolitan Boston Transportation Authority. The "T," as the public transit system is known here, has five color-coded lines: Red, Green, Yellow, Blue, and Orange. If you remember a single rule, you'll have little trouble navigating the T: "inbound" trains are headed toward Park Street station, while "outbound" trains are moving away from it. The Purple Line (same phone number), or Commuter Rail, extending some 60 miles into the suburbs, is handy for longer trips. Visitor T passes for one day ($6), three days ($11), or seven days ($22) are sold at major stations, but the new **weekly combo pass** ($12.50 per week) may be a better value for you. Valid Sunday to Saturday, it gives the bearer bus, subway, and inner-city Commuter Rail privileges. It's available at Harvard Square, Kenmore, Haymarket (Green Line), Park Street (Green Line, outbound only), Government Center, and other stations. Also, note that MBTA buses now offer free transfers.

Most air travelers arrive in Boston at **Logan International Airport** (617-428-2800), but there are alternatives in the form of excellent regional airports: Hartford (860-292-2000), Burlington (802-863-2874), Manchester (603-624-6556), Portland (207-774-7301), Providence (888-268-7222), and Worcester (888-FLY-WORC, 359-9672). Information on these smaller airports is available through Massport (www. massport.com) and Fly New England (www.flynewengland. com).

Acela is the high-speed service of **Amtrak** (South Station, 617-345-7460, www.amtrak.com) between Boston and Washington, DC, traveling at a top speed of 150 mph. The train, which also serves Baltimore, Philadelphia, New York, New Haven, and Providence, stops at three stations in the Boston area: Route 128, Back Bay, and South Station.

SECRET
ACCENT

Like "a brick-throated bullfrog," was how writer Ford Maddox Ford described the Boston accent, noting that on hearing it "the Almighty . . . must bitterly have regretted He ever invented the vocal organs of humanity." Ouch.

Still, many Boston subway riders expressed regret a few years back when MBTA conductors' live announcements of upcoming stops from "Hah-*vid*!" to "Pahk!" were replaced by a crisp recording. Something was lost that day.

If you want to pass yourself off as a local, it's not enough to pahk your Rs in Hahvid Yahd. Abbreviations are key. Never say the Prudential Center, the Museum of Fine Arts, Massachusetts Avenue, Commonwealth Avenue, Jamaica Plain, Memorial Drive, or (gawd-fahbid) Dorchester Avenue. Instead say the Pru, the MFA, Mass Ave, Comm Ave, JP, Mem Drive, and Dot Ave. You may never be a brick-throated bullfrog, but at least you won't sound like a tourist.

SECRET
AFRICAN-AMERICAN

From 1630, when Puritans settled there, through its development in the mid-1800s as a working-class Irish neighborhood, to its present incarnation as the heart and soul of Boston's African-American community,

Roxbury weaves a fascinating story. Long neglected by outsiders, this neighborhood has begun welcoming visitors who come to explore Roxbury's colonial-era sites as well as its superb traditional African and contemporary Afro-centric cultural offerings. One of the boosters in the push to rejuvenate Roxbury is Dudley Square Main Streets (617-541-4644). The organization has developed **historic walking tours** that take in such diverse sights as the home of Malcolm X and the 1750 Dillaway-Thomas House (Roxbury Heritage State Park, John Eliot Square, Roxbury, 617-445-3399), a Revolutionary War headquarters. The tours were under development at the time of research; call for an update.

Well before the current Dudley Square renaissance began, the **Hamill Gallery of African Art** (2164 Washington Street, 617-442-8204) was already here. "We show traditional African art," says owner Tim Hamill, "art that functions in the society and doesn't change." Recently expanded to three spacious floors, the gallery has a new front entrance on Washington Street (ring the bell), as well as a new outside mural by Kofi Kayiga. Inside, the walls of this former picture-framing warehouse are artfully covered with works of the tribes of central, western, and eastern Africa. From the Hemba tribe in the Democratic Republic of Congo, Hamill has procured a collection of wooden Suku helmet masks with serene faces perched over wild raffia collars. There are Kirdi beaded aprons, some with abstract designs and others describing landscapes, villages, and savanna; geometrically carved wooden granary doors made by the Dogon; and divination objects (trays, bowls, beaded bags) used by communities to communicate with their gods. Textiles range from brilliant Kente cloth (Ghana) to somber Pygmy bark cloth (Zaire). There are, as well, a few less expensive gift-type items. Hamill has put together a wide-ranging library of books on African art, set up as an informal reading room in the upstairs gallery. Anyone can stop and read, and many of the books are also available for purchase. Open Wednesday to Saturday (noon to 6 PM) and by appointment. There is a free enclosed parking lot off Eustis Street.

Not far from Tim Hamill's place, CK **African Art Market** (155 Dudley Street, 617-427-2090) is a packed shop devoted, in part, to African imports. Cire Kaba, from Guinea, may be busy braiding hair (another of her enterprises), but that won't stop her from offering to "give you a good price." Look for antique masks, brightly dyed African clothing, carved musical instruments, Kente cloth, and mud cloth (so called because its patterns are dyed with river mud) for wall hangings. Open Monday to Saturday (10 AM to 6 PM).

Anyone in the market for contemporary Afro-centric and Caribbean goods can stop in **A Nubian Notion** (44–47 Warren Street, 617-442-2622), where vivid posters, cosmetics, chunky jewelry, CDs — including recordings by local talent — and cards are for sale. At **African Market** (2285 Washington Street, 617-427-7131), proprietor Hassan Aboagye-Marfo sells African shirts and CDs you won't find anywhere else in the city, as well as African specialty foods.

Housed in an 1870s Roxbury puddingstone mansion, the **Museum of the National Center for Afro-American Artists** (300 Walnut Avenue, 617-442-8614) is the only museum in New England dedicated to African, Caribbean, and African-American fine arts. Rotating exhibits feature paintings from the collection, including James Reuben Reed's evocative portraits of black women of Boston. On permanent display, a Nubian burial chamber replica complete with hieroglyphics and massive sarcophagus brings ancient African art into the context of this contemporary art museum. The mansion that houses the museum is one of the city's best examples of Victorian neo-Gothic architecture. Open Tuesday to Sunday (1 PM to 5 PM).

A number of Roxbury art events are sponsored throughout the year by ACT **Roxbury** (2201 Washington Street, Suite 300, 617-541-3900, ext. 222). In August, the **Roxbury Film Festival** brings feature-length films, documentaries, and shorts by filmmakers of color to Northeastern University. The annual **Roxbury Open Studios** event takes place in early October. ACT also puts on **Roxbury in Motion**, an annual performing arts event, and produces the *Roxbury Literary Annual*.

When Roxbury was still a vast apple orchard, Beacon Hill was home to a large community of African-Americans. Headquartered in the 1806 African Meeting House and Abiel Smith School, the **Museum of Afro-American History** (46 Joy Street, at Smith Court, 617-725-0022) presents the history of New England's colonial-era African-American community. There are changing exhibits at the meeting house; at the Abiel Smith School, a video details the story of New England's black community and an interactive computer program offers a virtual encyclopedia of black history. The school also has a shop selling African toys and textiles, and books on black history and heroes. From Memorial Day to Labor Day, open daily (10 AM to 4 PM); closed Sundays in winter; $5.

The Museum of Afro-American History is one of a dozen or so sites along the 1.6-mile **Black Heritage Trail**, which follows the history of Boston's 19th-century African-American community. The Boston African American National Historic Site (617-742-5415, www.nps.gov/boaf) does excellent guided tours of the trail, painting a picture of life on the backside of Beacon Hill before the Civil War. Because many of the sites along the trail are private residences, because Beacon Hill's demography is so changed, *and* because so much of black history has been overlooked for so long, a guide is all but essential. He or she will not only review the history of the area, but will regale you with stories of the people who lived and congregated here. You'll hear of free blacks, escaped slaves, abolitionists, fallen Civil War heroes, and even a barber whose shop doubled as a rendezvous for runaway slaves.

You may also hear the riveting story of Ellen and William Craft, who escaped from slavery in Georgia in 1848 by posing as a white man (Ellen) and his slave (William). Safely arrived in Boston, the couple settled down and quickly became popular speakers on the abolitionist circuit. When Congress passed the Fugitive Law in 1850, Beacon Hill friends harbored the Crafts. The couple evaded their would-be captors, partly because abolitionist Lewis Hayden (also an escaped slave) threatened to detonate two kegs of dynamite under his Phillips Street porch. The **home of Lewis and Harriet Hayden** (66 Phillips Street), a private residence, is another stop on the trail.

SECRET
ANATOMY

The library staff calls him "Nosferatu" — he gazes down sunken-eyed from a framed daguerreotype, his spidery fingers grazing the top of a skull. Meet John Collins Warren (1778–1856), eminent Victorian physician and founder of the **Warren Anatomical Museum** (Countway Library, 10 Shattuck Street, next to Brigham and Women's Hospital, 617-432-4888), a cabinet of curiosities on the fifth floor of Harvard Medical School's Countway Library.

In an era when human dissection was illegal, Warren and other teaching physicians relied on grave robbers to find specimens for their lectures. To turn these cadavers into teaching tools, Warren treated the specimens at his home on Park Street, separating limbs, stripping away flesh, injecting veins and arteries with colored wax and leaving his handiwork to air dry on a windowsill. His housekeeper considered the whole business so creepy that she once refused to return until the doctor tidied up.

Today these air-dried extremities are among the museum's array of 15,000 anatomical artifacts. Newly installed in the Countway Library after languishing elsewhere on campus for decades, a small sampling of the full collection now appears in changing exhibits.

Many people have contributed objects to the museum over the years. One of the donors was Oliver Wendell Holmes, who bestowed a collection of microscopes, as well as the skeletons of an eagle and a woodchuck. Others gave, literally, of themselves. Notes appended to the museum's storehouse of amputated limbs state such sentiments as "I hereby donate my leg. . . ." There are decorated lancet cases with sharkskin and tortoiseshell covers; bladder, gall, and kidney stones (the museum has some 1,000 of them in all), cut open like geodes to reveal multi-hued layers; skeletons of conjoined ("Siamese") twins; and lurid watercolor paintings showing the effects of gangrene.

The most famous of the Warren's artifacts is the skull of the "crowbar man," Phineas Gage, whose ordeal provided science with its first real understanding of the brain. Born in 1823, Gage was a railroad construction foreman in the mid-1840s. One day he miscalculated while preparing a blast and the ensuing explosion sent a yard-and-a-half-long, 13-pound tamping iron through his head. Gage lost an eye and most of the part of his brain called the frontal lobe — an area we now know controls social functions. The once friendly and well-liked Gage became, according to his physician, "impatient, obstinate, fitful, irreverent and grossly profane." Too restless to keep a job, Gage traveled from place to place for the rest of his life, working odd jobs and eventually exhibiting himself, along with the fateful tamping iron, as a "freak" with P.T. Barnum. He died of an epileptic seizure in 1860 and was buried with the iron. Harvard eventually got permission to exhume the skull and iron in 1867.

When you visit the Warren, be sure to head down to the **Rare Books** department (Level LL2), where a small changing display features unusual books in combination with fascinating photographs and objects. Past exhibits have covered plastic surgery and phrenology.

The museum is open Monday to Friday (9 AM to 5 PM). Bring identification and sign in at the library's front desk; free. Parking is a chore in the Longwood Medical Area; best to take the Green Line Riverside branch to Longwood or the Heath Street branch to Brigham Circle. If you must drive, you'll likely have to pay for parking at one of the hospital lots.

SECRET

ANIMAL RESCUE

When Poomba the Cat strolled into the backyard with a bird in her teeth, my friend knew just what to do. She removed the warbler from the jaws of death, got a shoebox from the house, punched several holes in the box, filled it with grass and a strip of damp paper towel, and placed the stunned bird inside. Next day, she transported the patient to the **New England Wildlife Center** (19 Fort Hill Street, Hingham, 781-749-5387) where for $25 she secured an x-ray, a good prognosis and a promise to rehabilitate the little songbird. The center is open weekdays (9 AM to 5:30 PM) and weekends (10 AM to 2 PM).

An auxiliary to Tufts' School of Veterinary Medicine, **Tufts Wildlife Clinic** (200 Westboro Road, North Grafton, 508-839-7918) also doctors wild animals. If you find an injured creature — be it snake, turtle, chipmunk, or duck — give the clinic a call and the staff will walk you through the options. Like their counterparts at the Hingham clinic, Tufts' vets always aim to get animals back into the wild as soon as possible. They'll give you the option of retrieving the patient so you can release it where you found it. However, if you have any feline hunters about, you might want to let the clinic find a new wild home for it. Open weekdays (8 AM to 4 PM) and weekends (9 AM to noon). Tufts' services are free, though they do take donations. Ask Poomba if she cares.

SECRET
ANTIQUE MALLS

It was the three-foot-tall Art Deco letter "A" that caught my attention. A Hester Prynne accessory for the 21st century? At the **Massachusetts Antiques Cooperative** (100 Felton Street, Waltham, 781-893-8893), you never know what you'll discover. This antique mall consolidates the finds of around 100 dealers in two rambling buildings. Located down a semi-industrial side street in Waltham, the co-op has the standards — old furniture, sheet music, and dishes — as well as some outstanding art pottery and jewelry. On Sundays (10 AM to 11 AM), MAC dealers do free, walk-in appraisals. Closed Tuesdays.

In a similar vein, the **Cambridge Antique Market** (201 Monsignor O'Brien Highway, 617-868-9655) has around 150 dealers on five floors. Some of the objects in this brick warehouse near the Lechmere T station are merely old rather than antique. But whatever you choose to call them, they are legion. Look not for Louis XV. Rather, keep an eye peeled for stacks of Fiestaware, working 1960s Ericophones, novelty salt and pepper shakers, etchings, and the astounding wall o' wood planers. Trek to the basement for furniture; visit the top floor for a 21st-century snack. The market is open Tuesday to Sunday (11 AM to 6 PM); there's a small parking lot that fills early.

SECRET
ARCHITECTURE

The Hub has its post-modern skyscrapers, but the best of Boston architecture captivates onlookers at street level, where Federal, Greek Revival, Victorian, and modern buildings embrace passersby with geniality and grace.

One of the city's most recognizable landmarks, the gold-domed "new" **State House** (Beacon Street, 617-727-3676) was built in 1798 by Charles Bulfinch (replacing the Old State House of 1713, which still stands on Washington and State streets; see "Secret Patriots"). It's been much modified, but the original structure with its red brick walls, graceful portico, and white pillars remains the centerpiece. Volunteer docents offer tours of the State House from Monday to Saturday (10 AM to 3:30 PM); free. I wouldn't call the tour a priority unless the Halls of Power make you go weak in the knees. Do pay homage, however, to the Sacred Cod (see "Secret Cod"), which hangs in the House of Representatives.

Soon after the appearance of the new State House, a host of Boston Brahmins commissioned its self-taught architect to design their **Beacon Hill homes**. "Within a dozen years," writes local historian Thomas O'Connor, "[Park Street and Tremont Street were] in the midst of rapid development, transforming the old Puritan town of wood and thatch into a new Federal capital of stone and granite." For a liberal dose of Beacon Hill style, visit Mt. Vernon Street, where practically all the houses are Federalist, many built by Bulfinch or his contemporaries. Here and all about the Hill, look for delicate wrought iron ("black lace") balconies; detailed doorways; and bow fronts hinting at a typical Federalist interior feature — lovely oval dining rooms. On Beacon Street, numbers 39 and 40 are Bulfinch houses with a peculiar detail. The windowpanes (also found at numbers 63 and 64), which came from England in 1818, contain a chemical that turns purple when exposed to sunlight. And so a faulty product became a priceless part of the Beacon Hill streetscape.

One of Bulfinch's finer residential dwellings, the 1796 **Harrison Gray Otis House** (141 Cambridge Street, 617-227-3956), is a feisty West End survivor of the bulldozing urban renewal program of the 1970s. Harry, the third mayor of Boston, made his pile through real estate speculation on Beacon Hill. This was his and his wife Sally's "starter home" (Bulfinch later built two other homes for them on the Hill). Reflecting the changing fortunes of the West End, the house became a Turkish bath in the 1830s, then a patent medicine shop, followed by a ladies' boarding house. Today, the Society for the Preservation of New England Antiquities has its headquarters here and has carefully restored the Federal interiors. The Society also maintains a small library on the premises (fee charged to nonmembers), as

well as a gift shop. Tours of the house take place on the hour, Wednesday to Sunday (11 AM to 5 PM); $4.

Next door, the **Old West Church** (131 Cambridge Street, 617-227-5088) has an 1806 design by Asher Benjamin, another influential Federalist architect inspired by the classic styles of late Georgian England. In the North End, the contemplative, white on white **St. Stephen's Church** (401 Hanover Street, no telephone number available) is the last surviving Boston church designed by Bulfinch.

Copley Square in the heart of the Back Bay is bounded by two of the most architecturally significant buildings in the United States: the Boston Public Library and Trinity Episcopal Church.

The **Boston Public Library** (BPL) — not the modern Philip Johnson wing along Boylston Street, but the Florentine Renaissance Charles McKim edifice facing Dartmouth Street — was built in 1895. This "palace of the people" was America's first major free public library, conceived as a place where people could not only read books, but also learn about beauty and form simply by being inside it. One hundred years later the ideals of its founders remain true, but the story of the BPL is a kind of reverse "Emperor's New Clothes." Bostonians tend to think the building is naked when, in fact, it's dressed in the most magnificent robes. **Art and Architecture Tours** (Dartmouth Street, Copley Square, 617-536-5400, ext. 2216) will knock the scales from your eyes. Tour guides point out the bare-breasted nymphs adorning Daniel Chester French's massive bronze doors; the mosaic vaulting where Very Important Bostonians, from artists to abolitionists, are commemorated; and the golden Viennese marble staircase guarded by Louis Saint-Gaudens' marble lions. The Delivery Room was modeled after a Venetian palace; once the place where readers picked up requested books, the chamber has a wrap-around mural by Edwin Austin Abbey, depicting the search for the Holy Grail in romantic, pre-Raphaelite style. On the third floor is John Singer Sargent's multi-paneled mural, *The Progress of Religion*. The library's colonnaded courtyard, designed by McKim to resemble the Palazza della Cancelleria at the Vatican, has been rebuilt from scratch after a serious flood. To the delight of many, *Bacchante and Infant Faun*, by Frederick MacMonnies, has finally taken its intended place in the center of the new courtyard. The statue was rejected by 19th-century trustees of the library, who thought it too risqué. Tours are offered Mondays (2:30 PM), Tuesdays and Thursdays (6 PM), and Fridays and Saturdays (11 AM).

Exiting the library onto Copley Square, you are in front of the rough-hewn form of **Trinity Episcopal Church** (Copley Square; for tour information, call the Trinity Church Bookstore, 617-927-0038), built by Henry Hobson Richardson in 1877. This Romanesque masterpiece was commissioned by Reverend Phillips Brooks (otherwise remembered for writing the words to the Christmas carol, "O Little Town of Bethlehem"). The building has become so popular that its custodians have started charging admission ($3) for those who come to gawk and not to bend a knee. It's a small price to pay for a peek at the magnificent interior, where the broad sanctuary glimmers in shades of earthy terracotta and green trimmed with shining gold leaf. Stained-glass windows on the north transept, with their vivid colors and organic designs, are from the workshops of William Morris & Co. The church schedules several guided tours each week. A leaky roof has forced a five-year restoration project, so visitors may find the church in scaffolding; call for an update.

A final notable on Copley Square is the soaring **Hancock Place**. Designed by Henry Cobb of the firm of I.M. Pei & Partners, the skyscraper joined Trinity and the BPL on the square in 1977. In order to avoid dominating the building's distinguished neighbors with its massive scale, Cobb attempted to make it "invisible" by constructing the exterior out of thousands of reflecting windowpanes. And, in fact, the skyscraper's best feature is considered by many to be the way it reflects neighboring Trinity Church — a classic Boston snapshot.

Cambridge has its fine old buildings, too, but the moderns stand out. On the Harvard University campus, the Carpenter Center (1961) is the only building in North America designed by the Swiss architect Le Corbusier. Housing the Harvard Film Archive (see "Secret Movies"), this rather modest building of poured concrete, pencil-like pillars, and a curving exterior ramp makes its best impression lit up at night. Harvard also has a number of notable old buildings, such as Massachusetts Hall (1720) and a couple of H.H. Richardson signatures (Sever Hall, Austin Hall).

At the neighboring **Massachusetts Institute of Technology** (MIT), landmark modern buildings abound. *Art and Architecture at MIT: A Walking Tour of the Campus*, available at the MIT Press Bookstore (292 Main Street, Cambridge, 617-253-5249) or the List Visual Arts Center (20 Ames Street, Cambridge, 617-253-4680) will guide you. Among other places, you can explore Alvar Aalto's curvilinear Baker Dormitory (1948); Eero Saarinen's bug-like Kresge Auditorium (1955), with its gorgeous wood-paneled hall; and Saarinen's tubular Kresge Chapel (1955), where hidden windows reflect light from a surrounding moat onto undulated interior walls.

The latest addition to MIT's campus could give an architecture buff goose bumps on her goose bumps: in 2003, the school will inaugurate its new Stata Center, a free-form complex designed by Frank O. Gehry. Not to be outdone, Harvard has hired Renzo Piano to contrive a new art museum. And, over the river again, Sir Norman Foster is designing the new wing of the *Museum of Fine Arts* (see "Secret Pictures"), and the *Institute of Contemporary Art* has enlisted Diller + Scofidio for its proposed new site at Fan Pier (see "Secret Art").

A high point for modernists is the pilgrimage west of the city to the **Gropius House** (68 Baker Bridge Road, Lincoln, 781-259-8098), home of the father of modern architecture. Bauhaus founder Walter Gropius came to Harvard to take the reins of the Graduate School of Design in 1937 and shortly thereafter built his home in Lincoln. Finished in 1938, the Gropius House was the first modern residence in New England and one of the first in the United States. Using pre-fab materials — the kitchen cabinets are designed for a chemistry lab — and Machine Age colors, Gropius managed to create a warm and harmonious environment. The furnishings and art are straight out of the Bauhaus workshops: tubular metal and canvas chairs by Marcel Breuer, Kandinsky murals. Call for hours; $8.

With the works of so many great architects in our midst, the *Museum of Fine Arts* (465 Huntington Avenue, 617-369-3395) offers two-hour architectural tours of Beacon Hill and the Back Bay from March to October ($25). But for the adventurous building admirer, the pinnacle is **Boston by Bike at Night**'s annual, mid-August, midnight-to-dawn bicycle tour of Boston's architecture and history (Back Bay Midnight Peddlers, 617-522-0259). Cyclists meet at 11:30 PM in front of *Trinity Church* in *Copley Square* with helmet, bike, lights, reflective clothing, and perhaps a bottle of Jolt Cola or two. The ride is free, but bring along $10 for a souvenir T-shirt.

SECRET
ARMENIAN

It languished for a quarter of a century in a Belmont church basement. Then, a decade ago, the **Armenian Library and Museum of
America** (65 Main Street, at Church Street, Watertown, 617-926-
2562) moved to its current home — a modern structure in the heart
of Watertown Square. Yet while its visibility has increased, only a
handful of non-Armenians know that this museum exists, and only a
tiny handful of these are aware of its treasures.

The open two-story plan of this former bank building provides an
ideal setting for the museum's marvelous collection of some 170 rugs
and kilims, displayed in rotation. Among the 7,000 objects that make
up the collection are a 15th-century illuminated Bible, coins and
stamps, religious art, lace, metalwork, and traditional costumes. Children can try their hand in the scriptorium, tracing letters from the
Armenian alphabet. Several galleries host changing exhibits of contemporary paintings, sculpture, and ceramics by Armenians.

On the second floor, the central exhibit tells the story of the system-
atic deportation and massacre of the Armenian people by the Turkish
government from 1915–1922. There is much to read, and the exhibit
succeeds in conveying the facts of the Armenian Genocide as well as
some part of the horror. Preserved here are the patched clothing and
wooden sandals of a boy who died of starvation on the forced march
to the Syrian Desert — found, too late, by international rescue workers — and a grainy photograph of a young Armenian slave with her
Turkish master's name tattooed across her chest and face. Above
these, and other objects and images, stand the words of Adolf Hitler in
1939: "Who today remembers the extermination of the Armenians?"

There are books available in the museum shop for those who want to know more about the rich culture and history of the Armenians. You can buy maps showing the former Armenian homelands, as well as CDs and tapes of traditional Armenian music, and jewelry. The shop also sells wonderful fabric dolls, handmade in Armenia. Each is dressed in leather shoes and a hand-knit vest or red velveteen dress and apron. The faces are embroidered and the male dolls sport proud black woolen mustaches and conical hats made of curly lamb's hair, while the women have printed scarves.

Look for museum-sponsored concerts and other events, usually free. Open Tuesdays (1 PM to 5 PM and 7 PM to 9 PM), Fridays and Sundays (1 PM to 5 PM); $2.

While the Armenian museum is little known outside the Armenian community, scores of non-Watertonians make regular pilgrimages to the shops lining Watertown's Mt. Auburn Street, which sell flavors imported from Egypt, Lebanon, Syria, Turkey, and Saudi Arabia.

The largest of these Armenian shops is **Massis** (569 Mt. Auburn, Watertown, 617-924-0537), where neat stacks of dried fruits — from the humble raisin to whole dried lemons and sumac berries — line the aisles. Dried legumes (fava beans, lentils, peas) are packed in clear containers. At the "olive bar," 14 types of olives swim in pungent pools. Lamejun (a thin round of soft bread covered with spiced minced meats and vegetables) is a house specialty. Massis makes it with beef or chicken, and even stocks a vegetarian version. At the deli counter, there are wheels of cheeses from Egypt, Hungary, Bulgaria, Lebanon, Syria, and Greece, while the bakery serves up honey-flavored sweets and breads. For those who don't know where to begin with all this bounty, there are Middle Eastern cookbooks.

Nearby, **Arax** (585 Mt. Auburn, Watertown, 617-924-3399) offers a similar line of foodstuffs in the context of a certain lovable chaos.

There's more in the way of kitchen equipment here than at Massis, and anyone in the market for a hookah should look no further.

Further down the street, **Sevan** (598 Mt. Auburn Street, Watertown, 617-924-9843) has long been my favorite place to buy muhammara, a rich red spread made from pomegranate molasses, cumin, pine nuts, bread crumbs, and "enough olive oil to soak the crumbs." It's sold by the pound. Food of the gods. Also in this snug shop are many of the same ingredients sold at the other stores, along with a very good bakery and a resplendent nut bar with bins of salted or unsalted filberts, pistachios, almonds, pecans, brazil nuts, macadamias, and cashews.

S E C R E T
ART

Before there was a Museum of Fine Arts (see "Secret Pictures"), there was the **Boston Athenaeum** (10 1/2 Beacon Street, 617-227-0270). Established in 1805 when a group of Boston men got together to edit a literary review, the Athenaeum — now approaching its 200th birthday — is America's oldest cultural institution. Two years after its founding the Athenaeum expanded, becoming a reading room, library, and museum for paying members. In 1849, the present Italianate building overlooking the Old Granary Burying Ground was inaugurated. A Vermont sheep farmer, Edward Clarke Cabot, had won a competition for its design.

Much of the Athenaeum's original art collection went to the Museum of Fine Arts when it opened in 1876. What remained forms the Athenaeum's present collection of 19th-century American art. Works include Jean Antoine Houdon's busts of Washington, Lafayette, and Franklin; Chester Harding's painting of Daniel Webster; and 20th-century African-American artist Allan Crite's *Harriet and the Lion*. You'll also find paintings by John Singer Sargent and Gilbert Stuart. In addition to its pictures and patriotic busts, the Athenaeum houses George Washington's personal collection of books, each with his bookplate and signature.

The Athenaeum remains a membership-based institution, but the art gallery is open to the public, weekdays (9 AM to 5:30 PM) and weekends (9 AM to 4 PM). Free tours of the building are available on Tuesdays and Thursdays (3 PM), or by appointment; reservations are required. During renovations, the Athenaeum will be closed; call for an update.

Collectively, the three **Harvard University Art Museums** (617-495-9400) own 150,000 objects ranging from ancient to modern. The Fogg (32 Quincy Street, Cambridge) has European and North American art from the Middle Ages to the present. It boasts a superb collection of early Renaissance Italian paintings, as well as a group of Impressionist and post-Impressionist works that includes pieces by Monet, Van Gogh, Renoir, and Picasso. It also has one of the world's largest collections of John Singer Sargent paintings. The Busch-Reisinger (enter through the Fogg) features the arts of German-speaking cultures, with German Expressionists predominating. The Sackler (485 Broadway, Cambridge) has ancient Asian, Islamic, and Indian art ranging from Buddhist cave-temple sculptures to bronzes, as well as Chinese jades and Asian woodblock prints. Open Monday to Saturday (10 AM to 5 PM), and Sundays (1 PM to 5 PM); $5. Harvard's art museums offer free admission on Wednesdays (10 AM to 5 PM) and Saturdays (10 AM to noon). General tours are offered Monday to Friday from September to June as follows: Fogg (11 AM), Busch-Reisinger

(1 PM), and Sackler (2 PM). In addition to these three museums, the Sert Gallery (Carpenter Center, next door to the Fogg) mounts exhibitions of modern and contemporary art.

Works from Europe, Asia, and the Americas at the **McMullen Museum of Art** (Boston College, Devlin Hall, 140 Commonwealth Avenue, Route 30, Chestnut Hill, 617-552-8100) span several centuries, from the 16th to the 20th. If you're willing to travel a bit, Andover has the **Addison Gallery of American Art** (Phillips Academy, Andover, 978-749-4015), with 12,000 art objects ranging from the paintings of John Singleton Copley to those of Frank Stella. Wellesley's **Davis Museum and Cultural Center** (Wellesley College, 106 Central Street, Wellesley, 781-283-3382) displays a number of concurrent exhibitions along with its permanent collection of European, American, African, and Asian art. Admission to these three school museums is free.

Set in the cramped quarters of an 1880s fire station, the **Institute of Contemporary Art** (955 Boylston Street, 617-266-5152) is scoping out a new 60,000-square-foot space at Fan Pier, South Boston, slated to open by 2004. It's still speculation at this point, but the architects have been chosen (Diller + Scofidio), and the new space is already taking shape in some minds, complete with a performance theater, media center, shop, and restaurant. Until then, the ICA continues to bring local, national, and international contemporary art and artists to its Back Bay quarters. It mounts changing exhibits in all media, including film festivals, installations, and performance art. Open Wednesdays and Fridays (noon to 5 PM), Thursdays (noon to 9 PM), and weekends (11 AM to 5 PM); $6.

While the ICA does not collect art, the **Rose Art Museum** (Brandeis University, 415 South Street, Waltham, 781-736-3434) does, boasting "the finest collection of 20th-century art in New England." Works date from the period following World War II and onward, with notable pieces by de Kooning, Johns, Rauschenberg, and Warhol; free.

Art on the Point (University of Massachusetts/Boston, Columbia Point, 617-287-5347) is an institution to watch as it acquires large-scale outdoor sculptures for a gorgeous, 200-acre hunk of seaside land. On the campus of UMass Boston, the sculpture park is open to the public daily year round. Further afield, the **DeCordova Museum and Sculpture Park** (Sandy Pond Road, Lincoln, 781-259-8355) vibrates with creative activity. The exhibitions are always worthwhile and the grounds are a changing landscape of monumental sculpture. Admission to the museum is $6; admission to the Sculpture Park is free.

SECRET
BAD ART

Located just outside the men's urinals in the leaky basement of the Dedham Community Theater, the **Museum of Bad Art** (580 High Street, Dedham, 617-325-8224) is devoted to collecting the worst art in the world. Founded in 1993, MOBA is the home of such seminal works as *Pablo Presley*, "a refreshingly multicultural treatment of one of the 20th century's most beloved icons;" *Nurds Descending a Staircase,* in which an army of purple Barneys marches into a peanut butter-colored hell; and the pastel-pointillist *Sunday on the Pot with George.*

In their mission to celebrate "the artist's right to fail gloriously," the curators have gone to great lengths to collect their treasures, rescuing them from trash heaps, tag sales, and cellars. If you feel the urge to take home a remembrance of this collection of art that is "too bad to be ignored," visit the upstairs refreshment counter, where MOBA T-shirts, CDs, and postcards are for sale. Open Monday to Friday evenings (6:30 PM to 10 PM), and weekends (1 PM to 10 PM). Admission is free and, as the museum's voice mail says, "worth every penny."

SECRET
BAKERIES

The clients at **Hi Rise Bread** (208 Concord Avenue, Cambridge, 617-876-8766) look like they're just up from the Cape. They're tanned, they're carefree, and they're entitled. In this case, they're taking for given a cornucopia of baked goods (puffy little gingerbread cakes, individual lemon meringue pies), baskets of crusty bread, fresh-cut sandwiches, and salads. And entertainment: beyond the rough wood tables where lunch happens is the bright arena of the baker's kitchen, with its vast ovens, mixers, prep tables, and bevy of bakers doing sadistic things to harmless rounds of dough. Hi Rise also offers take-home dinners (such as beef stew, roasted potatoes with fennel, and green beans almondine), wine, and a bread *du jour* (cheddar pepper, challah, walnut, raisin pear).

Iggy's Bread of the World has found its niche providing baked goods to cafés, gourmet food shops, and restaurants all over New England. But to get the full Iggy's experience, to see the full and awesome Iggy's line, to find out what goes into your Iggy's, and to get a cup of Iggy's organic coffee, you must go to the source. Iggy's retail outlet (205 Arlington Street, Watertown, 617-924-0949) is located in a Watertown warehouse. It's not a café, just a sunny hole-in-the-wall for all things Iggy — though you can enjoy your coffee

and cranberry pecan roll or sesame seed ficelle or raisin bagel or chestnut-paste-filled croissant on the shady loading dock, if you like. Iggy's ingredient list lets discriminating eaters know what they're consuming. It's all good: kalamata olives, caraway seeds, wheat flour, organic eggs, filtered water. The shop also carries a small selection of cheeses and teas. And they do about a dozen different sandwiches on their famous breads. Open every day.

While Iggy's croissants are superb, the choicest crescent-shaped pastries are baked at **Quebrada** (208 Massachusetts Avenue, Arlington, 781-648-0700). The almond croissant, oozing dollops of custard, must weigh in at about a quarter pound, so I wouldn't call it authentic. The word "luscious" comes to mind. The pain au chocolat is light on the outside and, on the inside, *riche, mystérieux, onctueux* (did I mention Quebrada's croissants cause you to start speaking French?). I've not seen the variety Quebrada offers elsewhere, either. In addition to the classics, there are cinnamon almond croissants, veggie versions (mushroom, spinach, broccoli), fruit-filled numbers (raspberry, apricot), and, finally, ham and cheese, cheese, and — for purists — "plain" croissants.

Kupel's (421 Harvard Street, Brookline, 617-566-9528), long famous for its great bagels, also has delicious hamentaschen and ruggelach pastries filled with cinnamon and chocolate, raspberry, apricot, raisins and so on, as well as plump rounds of rye bread, lustrous twists of challah, and more. Sandwich fixings and cold drinks make Kupel's both a breakfast and lunch oasis. Closed Saturdays.

Here's a secret for bakery bargain hunters: the otherwise fairly unremarkable **Marché Mövenpick** (Prudential Center, 800 Boylston Street, or enter on Belvidere Street, 617-578-9700) moves its baked goods — made on the premises — at two for one prices every night (7 PM to 10 PM).

SECRET

BARBECUE

I once spotted Steve Tyler from the band Aerosmith at **Redbones** (55 Chester Street, Somerville, 617-628-2200). Okay, who cares about celebrity sightings; let's talk barbecue. Let's talk slow-cooked Memphis-style barbecue. For some Redbones regulars (perhaps including old Steve), only a row of the eponymous "red bones," or ribs, will do. Get them dressed with mild, hot, sweet, or vinegar sauce, along with tasty sides of corn on the cob, beans, and slaw. If you can do without the bones, opt for a pulled-pork or fried catfish sandwich, preceded by some devilish "buffalo" shrimp with blue cheese dipping sauce. Redbones' beer is plentiful (with more than 50 varieties on tap); its lemonade, tangy and ice-cold, is served in tall mason jars. In the interest of promoting clean air, this Davis Square institution has a bicycle valet for anyone arriving on two wheels. Plus, Redbones serves a limited late night menu (10:30 PM to midnight). You can't get the works after 10:30 PM, but you can chow down on sandwiches and sides.

A different quadruped altogether can be found just outside Central Square. The **Cambridge Deli & Grill** (90 River Street, Cambridge, 617-868-6740) is largely unknown outside its loyal local clientele. And it's closed on weekends. Visit on a weekday for Texas-style barbecued ribs or, my pick, a perfectly grilled chicken breast fillet topped with BBQ sauce and nestled in a cuddly roll. Everything on the long menu is available for take out, but I like to eat in the small dining area with its wall-to-wall knotty pine paneling and tin ceiling.

SECRET
BEACHES

Boston's harbor cleanup has given back to its denizens a dozen or so of their beloved beaches. Lining the shore from Winthrop to Wollaston, many of these urban beaches are newly landscaped with fresh sand and picnic areas, as well as all sorts of other beach-going necessities, from clam shacks to chair rentals.

While city officials are doing a fine job with the sand, they can't do anything about the temperature of the water, which arrives on our shores freshly chilled from somewhere in the vicinity of Reykjavik. (The average temperature in summer is just under 70 degrees Fahrenheit.) At **Pleasure Bay Beach**, the enclosing Castle Island Causeway holds cold ocean currents somewhat at bay, making the waters here warmer than most area beaches. But truly, for a swim in the sea that won't knock off your knickers, you'll have to go to Rhode Island (but that's another book). That said, cold water doesn't stop a genuine Yankee from a plunge. And anyway, Boston beaches have become so inviting that even wimps like me enjoy going just for the sun and salt air (and lobster rolls).

Hugging Boston's Old Harbor, a two-mile stretch of what have been called some of the best urban beaches on the East Coast runs along South Boston's shoreline. **Carson Beach** (accessible from the JFK/UMass T station) boasts the restored **McCormack Bathhouse** (165 Day Boulevard, South Boston) where the Ski Market's **kayak demo center** (617-464-3291; call for hours and prices) offers sea kayak rental by the hour or by the day. On the boardwalk, the **Beachside Café** (617-269-6973) is a neat little clam shack with nicely done fried seafood (fish and chips, clams, scallops, shrimp, oysters, and calamari), as well as chowder, sandwiches, and ice cream. It's open every day and there are shady café tables where you can take your haul. If that's not fresh enough, then fish for bass and bluefish (800-ASK-FISH, 800-275-3474) at the pier in front of the neighboring Bayside Expo Center.

Moving north along the seaside promenade you'll find the **Curley Community Center** (1663 Columbia Road, 617-635-5104), which any Massachusetts resident can join for a nominal fee to enjoy the private beach, sauna, steam room, and exercise classes. The Curley Center incorporates three 1930s bathhouses, including the L Street Bathhouse, home of the L Street Brownies, notorious for their New Year's Day plunge into the surf. Next to the Curley is the **M Street Beach**, a public facility. Very nice. In fact, I'd say it's nicer for swimming than Carson Beach, where a bit more gunk tends to wash up. But then Carson has the clams and kayaks. Your call.

Next on the strand is Pleasure Bay Beach (mentioned above), ringed by a gorgeous two-mile paved path leading out to **Castle Island** (Day Boulevard, 617-727-5290). There, you'll find supervised swimming areas, a fishing pier, and the Civil War-era **Fort Independence,** where you can take a guided tour on weekends during the summer; call the Castle Island number above for details. **Sullivan's** (617-268-5685) provides the burgers and fries (March to November). This windswept peninsula is a superb place to fly a kite. Pleasure Bay and Castle Island beaches have, depending on how you look at it, the added fascination or annoyance of being under the Logan International Airport flight path.

For these and all other urban beaches, the city monitors water quality and posts warnings if bacteria levels are high (usually after a heavy rain); reports are available from the **Metropolitan District Commission** (617-727-5264, ext. 517, www.magnet.state.ma.us/mdc/harbor. htm).

If you walk south from Carson Beach, you'll find a paved path all the way around Columbia Point to the **John F. Kennedy Library and Museum** (Columbia Point, 617-929-4523) and beyond.

Although Boston's inner-city beaches are bouncing back, five miles north of Boston **Revere Beach** is still a big draw for beach-goers. Established in 1896, Revere is the oldest public beach in the country. Once known as the Coney Island of New England, complete with carousels, roller coasters, cinemas, dance halls, and seaside hotels, today it's your basic strand of sand, celebrated for its parade of muscle shirts and string bikinis — and **Kelly's Roast Beef** (410 Revere Beach Boulevard, 781-284-9129). Open until 2:30 AM.

To the south of the city in Hull, **Nantasket Beach** is a wide stretch of golden sand and shallow water that's a delight for families with young children. This old-fashioned seaside is the kind of place where a brass band might come marching along the sand to play a little impromptu Dixieland concert. Along the boardwalk are burger and ice cream shacks, as well as the grand old **Paragon Carousel** (781-925-0472). It was built in 1928 and moved to Nantasket in the 1980s, along with its Wurlitzer organ. Open Wednesdays (10 AM to 1 PM), Fridays (3 PM to 6 PM), and weekends (11 AM to 6 PM).

The best seaside scenery, aside from Revere's flesh parade, is found on North Shore beaches. Expect a mix of frothy surf, white sand, rocky cliffs, and shorebirds at the following: **Singing Beach** (Manchester-by-the-Sea, 978-526-2000), which can be reached via the MBTA Commuter Rail; **Crane Beach** (Trustees of Reservations, Ipswich, 978-356-4351); and Gloucester's **Wingaersheek Beach** and **Good Harbor Beach** (Parks and Recreation, Gloucester, 978-281-9790).

SECRET

BIG DIG

Built in the 1950s to allow traffic to bypass downtown's gnarled streets, Boston's six-lane Central Artery, or "ahdery" as it's referred to locally, has been cursed ever since. First, it cut off the waterfront and North End from the rest of city; second, it was almost immediately obsolete. Designed to handle 75,000 cars a day, it would soon be carrying more than 200,000 vehicles a day, prompting the term "bumper to bumper" to become a routine part of the Boston lexicon.

Enter the **Big Dig**, the largest public works project in United States history. The Central Artery/Tunnel Project (the Dig's official name) is replacing the rusting elevated roadway, which will be demolished by 2004, with an 11-lane underground throughway. The $14.4-billion (and counting) project has given Boston a third harbor tunnel, the Ted Williams, connecting the mainland to Logan International Airport, and a graceful, 300-foot-tall, cable-stayed bridge called the **Leonard P. Zakim** or the **Bunker Hill Memorial**, depending who you talk to. Over the "depressed" artery, a system of parks and walkways has begun to spring up that will reunite the city's most historic neighborhoods — the North End, Charlestown, South Boston — with the city at large.

To help amateurs comprehend the complexity and vastness of an entity that has been called "the eighth wonder of the world," the CA/T Project sponsors **guided walking tours** (617-951-6400) throughout the summer. Of course, someday the Dig will be finished, but CA/T plans to continue the tours for the foreseeable future. Call or check the Web site (www.bigdig.com) for current information. Book well in advance; these tours are very popular. In addition to seeing the Dig in

person, you can visit an official Big Dig **exhibit** at 220 State Street and a **scale model** of the project at 185 Kneeland Street. Again, check the CA/T number before you go looking for anything related to the Big Dig as it is in continual flux.

Your explorations of the Central Artery will provide you with all the dirt on what goes into such a massive project. For a look at what comes out, visit the **Commonwealth Museum** (Massachusetts Archives Building, 220 Morrissey Boulevard, Columbia Point, 617-727-9268) for its ongoing exhibit on the archeological aspects of the Big Dig. Open Monday to Friday (9 AM to 5 PM), and Saturdays (9 AM to 3 PM); free.

While the new Artery is designed to accommodate 340,000 cars per day, naysayers claim it will soon be bumper to bumper. (Some Bostonians would have preferred that more money be diverted to public transportation.) Is the Big Dig the eighth wonder of the world, as its boosters proclaim, or just the earth's biggest temple to the almighty automobile? Time will tell.

SECRET
BIRDS
❋

During spring migration, birds flock to tree-laden **Mt. Auburn Cemetery** (Friends of Mt. Auburn Cemetery, 580 Mt. Auburn Road, 617-864-9646). Several groups offer guided birding expeditions around this 174-acre arboretum, including Friends of Mt. Auburn and the Massachusetts Audubon Society (800-AUDUBON, 800-283-8266). If you're going solo, stop at the entrance gate to check the sightings board and pick up a pamphlet listing recent sightings and locations. You should also purchase a map, as the grounds have 10 miles of trails. Similarly, **at Forest Hills Cemetery** (95 Forest Hills Avenue, Jamaica Plain, 617-524-0128), you can stop by the office for a free brochure called Birds of Forest Hills Cemetery, which details around 25 birds commonly spotted here, from buffleheads to wild turkeys. Both properties are open from dawn to dusk.

Besides these two long-time birding haunts, city birders have a new rendezvous at the **Boston Nature Center** (Massachusetts Audubon Society, 450B Walk Hill Street, 617-983-8500), a 67-acre wildlife sanctuary not far from Franklin Park. There are two miles of easy trails to explore here, as well as the Clark Cooper Community Gardens, which developed out of the gardens of a state mental hospital that once occupied this land. Look for hawks and wild turkeys, as well as scores of songbirds during migration periods. Open daily (9 AM to 5 PM).

Keep your eyes on the sky in mid-September, when **hawks**, heading south for their winter homes in South America, fly over eastern Massachusetts. In past years, hawk watchers have sighted broad-winged hawks hailing from local woods, goshawks from Quebec, peregrine falcons from Labrador, and an occasional golden eagle. You can watch for raptors wherever you happen to be: walk out the back door in your jammies and look up — badda-bing! But for prime viewing, head for the Blue Hills Reservation, where the Massachusetts Audubon Society's **Trailside Museum** (1904 Canton Avenue, Route 138, Milton, 617-333-0690, ext. 223) holds a fall hawk migration workshop in September. The observation deck of the Custom House Tower (see "Secret City Views") has posted articles and information on the tower's resident peregrine falcons (www.state.ma.us/dfwele/dfw), which have bred 36 chicks since they began nesting here several years ago. The **Eastern Massachusetts Hawk Watch** (781-648-3794) recruits volunteers to count raptors during peak migration periods. Call to find out how to participate.

Elsewhere around the city, there are scores of opportunities to spot birds and other wildlife. Paddle a canoe from Milton Landing on the **Neponset River Reservation** (Metropolitan District Commission, 617-727-8556) out to the harbor for sightings of shore birds, as well as harbor seals. Cruise the harbor on a whale watching trip (see "Secret Boston Harbor") and spot scores of pelagic birds. Walk along the Charles River at dusk with your eyes peeled for flocks of black-crowned night herons, which feed along the banks. Look for snowy egrets, black ducks, and shorebirds at **Belle Isle Marsh** (Metropolitan District Commission, Bennington Street, 617-727-5350), Boston's last remaining salt marsh. Further afield, **World's End** (250 Martin's Lane, Hingham, 781-821-2977) is a stunning peninsula of land where informal early-morning bird walks take place on Saturdays throughout the winter; and **Plum Island** (Friends of Parker River National Wildlife Refuge, Newburyport, 978-749-9647) is one of the East Coast's top birding spots.

SECRET

BOCCE

The rules are simple: Roll the little pallino down the 70-foot alley. Then bowl the three-pound bocce ball as close as possible to the pallino. The bocce coming closest to the pallino scores. There are 12 points in a game.

To see bocce — an Italian version of lawn bowling — played by the "pros," follow Hanover Street toward the waterfront to the three regulation **bocce courts** at Puopolo Park (Commercial Street, 617-635-4505), where you can follow this intense, social game while enjoying fresh breezes from the sea. Take a seat on a bench under the shade of young locust trees — front-row seats overlooking the sunken sand courts, or campos. The "audience" will usually include a handful of men of a certain age wearing wrap-around sunglasses. Down on the courts you'll find people of all ages and genders.

Polish your own game at the small, indoor court at **Bertucci's Pizzeria** (197 Elm Street, Somerville, 617-776-9241). Balls are provided.

SECRET
BOOKSTORES

Harvard Square is gentrifying fast, but this upscale acre is still one of the world's richest resources for book lovers. **WordsWorth** (1 JFK Street, Cambridge, 617-498-0062) is a general store with 100,000 or so titles in stock. It stays open later than most bookstores (Monday to Saturday until 9 PM, Sundays until 8 PM), and every paperback is between 10 and 35 percent off the publisher's price. The store also has a star-studded visiting author series. **Curious George Goes to WordsWorth** (at JFK and Brattle streets) is the shop's somewhat zany (i.e., crowded) kiddy lit annex. See below for some alternatives in that arena.

Among the more remarkable of the many specialized Harvard Square bookshops is **Schoenhof's Foreign Books** (76A Mt. Auburn Street,

Cambridge, 617-547-8855). Established in 1856, this cellar shop has sections in scores of languages devoted to literature, children's books, and essays, as well as a language-learning department with dictionaries, grammars, and tapes. Schoenhof's reference staff includes specialists in Spanish, French, Russian, and other modern languages. Ask them anything. For foreign periodicals, however, visit **Out of Town News** (Zero Harvard Square, Cambridge), where newspapers and magazines from dozens of countries are sold along with local and national periodicals.

Down a side street off Massachusetts Avenue, **Grolier Poetry Book Shop** (6 Plympton Street, Cambridge, 617-547-4648) is poetry itself, with its tall stacks of known, soon-to-be-known, and never-to-be known lyricists. It's the oldest poetry bookshop in the country, with 15,000 titles, as well as limited-circulation magazines and cassette tapes. Look for the store's autograph parties and other events. Open Monday to Saturday (noon to 6:30 PM).

For travelers, the **Globe Corner Bookstore** (28 Church Street, Cambridge, 617-497-6277) is tops, with topo maps, globes, atlases, language tapes and dictionaries, and a wide selection of travel guidebooks. It now has a branch in the Back Bay as well (500 Boylston Street, 617-859-8008).

Harvard Square has the area's last surviving Marxist bookstore, **Revolution Books** (1156 Massachusetts Avenue, 617-492-5443), selling all the necessary paraphernalia (T-shirts, bumper stickers) for the 21st-century Red.

There are at least 15 more booksellers in Harvard Square. For a complete list, contact the **Cambridge Office for Tourism** (800-862-5678), which distributes the Bookstore Guide, a free brochure. And if you're going to spend much time in Harvard Square, take note: while most people have discovered the once-secret bathrooms at the

Harvard Coop (1400 Massachusetts Avenue), not many people are aware of the public restrooms on the third floor of the Holyoke Center. Give them a whirl.

"To support women's writing and progressive change, regardless of market trends and corporate whims" is the out-loud mission of **New Words** (186 Hampshire Street, Cambridge, 617-876-5310). More than a regional intellectual landmark, New Words is one of the United States' largest and longest-running women's bookstores. Beyond the books, there is a well-rounded collection of CDs, magazines, and gift cards. Browse the bumper sticker binder for the appropriate tagline for your vehicle. Rent a video from the collection of women-centered titles ranging from Hollywood blockbusters to lesbian sleepers.

Gay, lesbian, bisexual, and transgender titles are the stock-in-trade at **Calamus Bookstore** (92B South Street, 617-338-1931). The hub of the South End's thriving gay community, **We Think the World of You Bookstore** (540 Tremont Street, 617-574-5000) is hailed as the best all-around gay bookstore in the city. It has a globetrotting travel section, as well as fun gifts. Open every day.

Also in the South End, the **Lucy Parsons Center** (549 Columbus Avenue, 617-267-6272) is grooving in a new South End home after being evicted from Central Square, Cambridge. In addition to stacks of labor-related titles, the center has posters, obscure political magazines, and T-shirts, and hosts Radical Movie Night each Wednesday (7 PM).

Jamaica Plain bookstores, like the neighborhood, defy categorization. The soulful **Jamaicaway Books & Gifts** (676 Centre Street, Jamaica Plain, 617-983-3204) sells books in the setting of a gallery of traditional and contemporary art and textiles from Africa and the East. In addition to a wide selection of multicultural books, including new releases, bestsellers, and books by African-American authors, there are printed note cards featuring the works of artists of color, such as Jacob Laurence and Frida Kahlo. A busy schedule of open mic poetry nights, readings, author appearances, seminars, and jazz concerts ($5 donation for concerts) makes this as much a community center as a shop. Also on JP's main drag, **Rhythm & Muse** (403A Centre Street, Jamaica Plain, 617-524-6622) takes a left-brain, right-brain approach to commerce. On one side of the shop are books and on the other, music. In the middle — the medulla oblongata, if you will — is a café with comfy couches and tables, and a coffee and pastry counter — an automatic invitation to stay and chat with whoever happens by and their dog (everyone in JP has a dog). Books by local authors and biographies of Boston luminaries take pride of place on the shelves.

Allow plenty of time for a trip to Ken Gloss's **Brattle Book Shop** (9 West Street, 617-542-0210). Before shoppers cross the threshold of this antiquarian bookshop, the display windows hold them spell-bound. There might be scrapbooks stuffed with lace fragments, leather-bound and gold-embossed libraries, books inscribed with marginalia by the famous, or an antique map of Boston. Just as distracting is the Brattle's bouquiniste-style sidewalk sale. It takes place (weather permitting) in a vacant lot next to the shop, with hundreds of used books for $1 to $3 each. Inside the two-story shop is a superb collection of old and rare books. Of particular note is the front-and-center aisle dedicated to books on New England, Massachusetts, Boston, and Cambridge, which includes everything from travelogues to the literary works of Emerson, Thoreau, and friends. You'll find just about everything here, but the shop's strengths are history and other nonfiction.

Another excellent old book mine is **Avenue Victor Hugo** (339 Newbury Street, 617-266-7746), set in a mid-19th-century row house. This shop has a robust sci-fi collection, both hardcover and paperback, but its towering shelves hold a little of everything, including periodicals of yesteryear. Across the street, **Trident Booksellers and Café** (338 Newbury Street, 617-267-8688) deals in new books and scores of periodicals. The owners, originally from Vermont, have adapted the Green Mountain State's easygoing attitude to fit their chic Back Bay digs. In the café, try the vegetarian cashew chili, a wheatgrass hopper drink, and a rich dessert. Service is lax, but who cares? You've got a book.

Newtonville Books (296 Walnut Street, Newton, 617-244-6619) is a welcome new addition to the Greater Boston book scene. It's small, but every precious square foot is packed with choice books. Employees are ready with smart assistance and their thumbnail reviews, tucked into their favorite titles, are helpful too. There's a couch to take your books for a test drive and, for kids, a little nook padded with a giant dog pillow. The frequent "shake the hand that pens the novel" readings feature talent from all over. And once a week or so, the reading and signing get really cozy when the whole group walks down to the Newtonville Times brew pub for appetizers (free) and ales (first round on the house).

Also in Newton, but occupying a different realm, is the **New England Mobile Book Fair** (82 Needham Street, Newton, 617-964-7440). Imagine being set loose in the warehouse of a major book distributor and you'll have an idea of the scope of this area institution. Bring a compass and C-rations; you might get lost for days. About two thirds of the floor space carries full-price books arranged, for the most part, under publishers and alphabetically by title — a baffling arrangement, but it has its charms. Highlights include a cookbook section that has earned the store several "Best of Boston" awards, as well as a vast — one might even venture to say "complete" — travel guide section showcasing every travel guidebook publisher known to humankind, and every country covered by each of those publishers. Still, the main attraction is the enormous "remaindered" section. Here, I've seen and bought books at 80 to 90 percent off the cover price that were still going for full price at other bookstores in town. There are employees wandering around if you need help and sets of *Books in Print* are available. The checkout line can drag on.

The **Children's Book Shop** (237 Washington Street, Brookline, 617-734-7323) has an excellent selection for kids in its small space, and the staff is always ready with suggestions of age-appropriate titles. **Jamaicaway Books & Gifts** (above) has children's books from all over the world, with emphasis on Africa. **Henry Bear's Park** (361 Huron Avenue, Cambridge, 617-547-8424) is a roomy and relaxed upscale toy store with a very nice kids' book department. While browsing, grown-ups can rest their tired selves on upholstered benches, and kids get just-right chairs.

SECRET
BOSTON HARBOR

Over the centuries, a lot has gone down, so to speak, in Boston Harbor: ships, pirates, English tea, not to mention tons of sewage and industrial waste. By the 1980s, so polluted was this historic body of water that it was named the nation's dirtiest harbor. Since then, a sweeping cleanup has begun, and though the project has years to go, Boston Harbor is on the rebound. Water quality has improved to the point that city beaches are re-opening (see "Secret Beaches"). Marine life is returning, too; observers have reported rising numbers of porpoises and harbor seals.

The heavyweight player in the harbor cleanup is the 212-acre **Deer Island Treatment Plant** (Massachusetts Water Resources Authority, 617-539-4248), where 12 giant egg-shaped "digestors" eat 350 million gallons of Boston's wastewater a day. The MWRA shows off its baby on tours of the plant. These take in the 130-foot-tall digestors, atop which visitors not only get great views of the skyline, but also a whiff of the "influents" the plant takes in and the "effluents" the plant produces.

Meanwhile, the official history of Boston Harbor can be heard on scores of harbor cruises, but only recently have we had a chance to hear and see the harbor's sunken treasure of tales. A new cruise called **Boston by Sea** (Boston Harbor Cruises, 617-227-4321) takes passengers on a 100-minute trip as musician David Coffin and actor Frank Ridley weave true tales of Boston's pirates and merchants (sometimes difficult to distinguish), sailors, slaves, and immigrants. During the trip, Coffin renders dozens of sea chanteys in his fine baritone, while Ridley dredges up forgotten historical characters like the "last living participant of the Boston Tea Party" and the men who rowed Paul Revere to Charlestown before his famous midnight ride. While the show keeps adults spellbound, there is plenty of fun for kids, who bounce up from their seats to raise the Jolly Roger, play powder monkey, and pretend to throw tea into the sea. Cruises run from early May to mid-October (11 AM and 1 PM); $19. Reservations recommended.

Camp overnight, take a hike in the dunes, woods, and salt marshes, go berry picking and sea kayaking, and, yes, take a dip in the sea. The **Boston Harbor Islands** (617-223-8666) offer all that and more. This urban archipelago is rich in geology, archaeology, history, and recreational possibilities. George's Island is the gateway to the harbor islands. You could spend a lazy day here exploring the tunnels and

ramparts of the Civil War-era **Fort Warren**, picnicking under the pines, fishing, playing volleyball, or doing a great deal of nothing. There's no better place (outside an air-conditioned shopping mall) to escape the heat wave that descends on Boston in August. Built of immense blocks of Quincy granite, the fort's tunnels and rooms stay cool even when the mercury reaches into the upper 90s outside. George's is a 45-minute trip from Long Wharf. From George's, you can continue by free shuttle boat to other islands.

From early May through Columbus Day weekend in October, you can pitch a camp in the **Boston Harbor Islands National Recreation Area** (617-223-8666). This is primitive, island camping; you must bring your own water, and the infrequent ferry schedule makes the sites too remote for regular visits to the city.

If sightseeing in Boston is on your agenda, you might try the campground at **Wompatuck State Park** (Union Street, Hingham, 781-749-7160). About a 15-minute drive from the park is Hewitt's Cove, where a commuter boat makes a short trip downtown, as well as to the harbor islands.

Also cruising out of the harbor, the **New England Aquarium** (Central Wharf, off Atlantic Avenue, 617-973-5200) offers excellent whale watch voyages to Georges Bank; and the **Friends of Boston Harbor Islands** (Long Wharf, 781-740-4290) do trips to Boston Light, America's first lighthouse, on Little Brewster Island. For a little romance, step aboard a tall ship called the **Liberty Schooner** (Boston Waterfront Marina, 67 Long Wharf, 617-742-0333). Cruises run daily (noon, 3 PM and 6 PM) from June to September.

Each spring, the **Boston Sailing Center** (The Riverboat at Lewis Wharf, 617-227-4198) invites would-be skippers to experience a free weekend of sailing. Call for dates. At other times, the center offers charters starting at $100 per hour. Set in a jewel of a park, **Piers Park Sailing Center** (Piers Park, 95 Marginal Street, 617-561-6677) has a terrific facility with a proud fleet of 23-foot sailboats. They have learn-to-sail programs for youths and adults from April to October, and season sailing passes for those who plan to sail regularly. To get your feet wet, try the three-hour introductory course ($45).

SECRET

BRAHMINS

It was Oliver Wendell Holmes who first used the term "Brahmin" to describe Boston's 19th-century aristocracy, with their "houses by Bulfinch, their monopoly of Beacon Street, their ancestral portraits and Chinese porcelains." While the Brahmin mystique has faded, a handful of homes-turned-museums offer visitors a look at the interior lives of this vaunted other half. These houses are stuffed with fine art and antiques, but their real fascination is the eccentric people who once lived in and preserved them. Visit, and surround yourself with the things that made their world.

The **Nichols House** (55 Mt. Vernon Street, 617-227-6993), an 1804 Bulfinch design, was the home of the Nichols family from 1885 until 1964, when it was bequeathed as a museum by Rose Standish Nichols. Miss Rose was a marvel. She *made* the carved oak chairs and the embroidered testers that hang on her four-poster bed. But those were just hobbies. Rose Nichols was a preeminent landscape architect, publishing in her lifetime three works on the subject and designing scores of gardens for wealthy New Englanders. She was also an outspoken advocate of social reform, one of the founders of the Women's International League of Peace and Freedom, and a tireless world traveler. In addition to the acquisitions and handiwork of Miss Rose, several generations of Nichols family possessions fill the house. There are the requisite ancestral portraits and Asian art, as well as 16th-century Belgian tapestries, Miss Rose's beloved French horticultural prints, and some exquisite works by Rose's Uncle "Gus," Augustus Saint-Gaudens. Miss Rose's afternoon teas were famous for their good conversation. In the cramped wood-paneled butler's pantry just off the dining room, contemporary visitors get an idea of the upstairs-downstairs nature of the period. Open May to October, Tuesday to Saturday (12:15 PM to 4:15 PM); November, December, and February to April, Mondays, Wednesdays, and Saturdays (12:15 PM to 4:15 PM); $5.

Edward Clark Cabot, who also designed the *Boston Athenaeum* (see "Secret Art"), built the **Gibson House** (Victorian Society, 137 Beacon Street, 617-267-6338) for wealthy matron Catherine Hammond Gibson in 1859. Most of the contents are original to the Gibsons, the only family ever to occupy the house. The last of the clan, Charles, began preserving elements of the house well before his death in 1954. He even roped off the furniture in his sitting room, leaving guests to sit on the stairs while sipping their tea. Early in the 20th century, few people saw the value in a crusty old Victorian house and its contents. But Charles knew that, say around the year 2000 or so, they'd come around. Today, visitors from all over the world come to see Charles Gibson's Victorian time capsule. Highlights include the entry hall with its Japanese faux-leather wallpaper and the 17-piece faux-bamboo bedroom set in the room where scenes from Henry James's *The Bostonians* were filmed. Open for tours Wednesday to Sunday (starting at 1 PM, 2 PM, and 3 PM); $5.

Just up the street is the **Prescott House** (National Society of the Colonial Dames, 55 Beacon Street, 617-742-3190), a swell-front beauty designed by Asher Benjamin in 1808, now owned and operated by the Colonial Dames. Its primary occupant was the historian W.H. Prescott, who wrote a history of the Spanish Empire. Blinded in a food fight while an undergrad at Harvard, Prescott went on to become an expert linguist. The apparatus he used for writing remains in his study. The house retains its original Asher Benjamin oval dining room, but the rest was remodeled in the 1870s in a light, bright neo-Colonial style — an interesting contrast to the brooding interiors of its contemporary, the Gibson House. Open for guided tours on Wednesdays, Thursdays, and Saturdays (noon to 4 PM) from mid-May to October; $5.

The Forbes family, Brahmins to the core, lived on Commonwealth Avenue but maintained a country estate in Milton (and another in Shanghai, for that matter). Built in 1833, **Captain Forbes's House** (215 Adams Street, Milton, 617-696-1815) is a resplendent Greek Revival mansion remarkable for its contents and very fine interior restoration. Captain Robert Bennett Forbes (1804–1889) was a China trade merchant. You won't hear about this on the house tour, but Forbes's nickname was "Black Ben"; like many Boston fortunes, Forbes's was built in part on the opium trade. The house, once the China Trade Museum (some maps still indicate it as such), is stuffed with Asian bounty: dozens of sets of Chinese dining porcelain, Chinese embroidery, carved rosewood furniture, and a fine portrait of the captain done by a Chinese painter who worked in Western style. Forbes's ancestors continued the collecting tradition. Mary Bowditch Forbes (the captain's granddaughter) was an admirer of Abraham Lincoln and for many years maintained a museum of presidential memorabilia on the grounds in a replica of Lincoln's birthplace. The log cabin remains (open by appointment), and the Lincoln collection is shown in temporary exhibitions at the big house. Open for tours Sundays and Wednesdays (1 PM, 2 PM, and 3 PM), and by appointment; $3.

The Forbes House is just three miles from the Adams National Historical Park in Quincy (see "Secret Patriots"). And across from the Forbes mansion is the 10-acre **Governor Hutchinson's Field** (Adams Street, Milton), all that is left of the country estate of a colonial governor of Boston. The meadow, cared for by the Trustees of Reservations (781-821-2977), has sweeping views of the Neponset River and Dorchester Bay and is a prime, undeveloped spot for birding, picnicking and cross-country skiing. Open dawn to dusk year round; free.

SECRET
BREAKFAST

Boston's best morning meeting places reflect the character of the neighborhoods they dwell in. In JP, expect funky rooms decorated with local art, the occasional Latin twist on the menu, and friendly service at **Sorella's** (388A Centre Street, 617-524-2016). Open 6:30 AM to 2:30 PM, every day. As a friend says, "There are so many ingredients in Sorella's omelettes, I don't know how they fit in the egg." The same thing goes for the **Centre Street Café** (see "Secret Cafés"), another superb JP breakfast feedbox. Served until 3 PM on weekends, breakfast choices include huevos rancheros, omelettes, and plate-sized pancakes flavored with unusual combos like pear and ginger.

The area around Tufts University, Somerville, is another morning microcosm. Arrive early on weekends or be prepared to stand in line.

Sound Bites (708 Broadway, Somerville, 617-623-8338) established the breakfast beachhead here a few years ago and continues to attract long lines of hungries on weekend mornings with its eggs, muffins, and items from the grill, frequently with tasty Middle Eastern twists. Nearby, representing Ball Square's blue-collar underpinnings, **Kelly's Diner** (682 Broadway, Somerville, 617-623-8102) serves classic chow to all walks of life. Over in Teele Square, **Renee's Café** (198 Holland Street, Somerville, 617-623-2727) is the best of these three. Recently expanded, more than doubling its dining space, this café is sunny and homey, and the plates of eggs anyway-you-like and nothing-fancy hotcakes are always fresh and nicely cooked. Service can be slow. Open Wednesday to Sunday (7 AM to 1:30 PM).

Some of us get up a little later, and to make up for our lack of enterprise, we call the morning meal "brunch." There are weekend brunches all over the city, but the South End scene has the most panache. **Claremont Café** (535 Columbus Avenue, 617-247-9001) has all the right ingredients: great food, reasonable prices, non-frumpy clientele, and sunny sidewalk tables. Club music tends to engulf the inside of the café, but it's a non-issue on sweet summer mornings, because everyone eats al fresco. Since my decision-making capacity is somewhat diminished of a morning, I welcome the "Claremont Combo" where French toast, scrambled eggs, and chorizo sausage intermingle in perfect three-part har-mo-ny ($9.95). Other than the smoked salmon platter, the combo is the most expensive item on the menu. In addition to Saturday (8 AM to 3 PM) and Sunday (9 AM to 3 PM) brunch, the café is open daily for breakfast ($1.50 to $8.50), lunch ($6.95 to $10.95), and dinner ($14.95 to $23.95).

Add music and you've got a jazz brunch. **Bob the Chef's** (604 Columbus Avenue, 617-536-6204) does it with a menu of soul food backed by a swing combo or a gospel choir on Sundays (10 AM to

2 PM). And in Cambridge, the **House of Blues** (96 Winthrop Street, Cambridge, box office, 617-497-2229) has its famous Gospel Brunch, when the house rocks with a display of religious fervor stoked by hominy grits and other Southern-inspired foods. Three seatings (10 AM, noon and 2 PM).

S E C R E T
BREWERY TOUR

Outside JP's Stony Brook T station, an idle smokestack towers over the Southwest Corridor Linear Park. The lettering reads: "FENREFFER." It's a vestige of the 17 breweries that once marinated the JP air. The last of the old breweries to close was Haffenreffer, former owners of that abbreviated smokestack.

Today the **Boston Beer Company** (30 Germania Street, 617-522-9080), makers of that really good beer called Samuel Adams, has poured new life into the old JP manufacturing mainstay. The brewery's testing labs are located here, and tours are offered to visitors, who arrive with a powerful thirst for knowledge and leave with a better understanding of how beer is made, along with a slight buzz. While waiting for the tour to start, you can browse an exhibit describing the history of beer from the Fertile Crescent to brewskies at Fenway. The exhibit also turns up some little-known facts. For example, Guinness Stout has a lower alcohol content than Miller Lite. Who knew? The tour takes visitors through the test brewery, where a series of vats are used to make beer from barley, yeast, hops, and water. Once the guide's spiel is over, it's on to the tasting room, a

mini beer hall where the steps of a professional beer taster are out-
lined. The day I visited, the final round of tasting involved black,
velvety cream stout. Lovely beer. But not everyone was convinced. "It
doesn't taste like beeyah," said a man next to me. "It's weeyud!" said
his wife. "Tastes like cawfee," they concluded. Not every Bostonian
has a taste for fine beer. After generous samples of three types of
Sam Adams beer, the gang is set loose in the gift shop. Tours take
place Thursdays (2 PM), Fridays (2 PM and 5:30 PM), and Saturdays
(noon, 1 PM, and 2 PM), with additional tours on Wednesdays (2 PM)
from May to August. A $2 donation goes to a local charity.

If you'd like to know more about the history of the German settlers
who once populated JP's Stony Brook area, contact the Jamaica Plain
Historical Society (617-524-5992) about its guided tours.

SECRET
CAFÉS

Run by the gentle, pony-tailed folks of Dorchester's Church of the
12 Tribes, the **Common Ground Café** (2243 Dorchester Avenue,
Lower Mills, 617-298-1020) is about as wonderfully offbeat as they
come. The café's interiors are fashioned out of raw wood, creating a
scene that is part English pub and part *A Midsummer Night's Dream.*
Cozy booths and gnarly tables incorporate woodland themes and,
yes, macramé (but it works!). On cooler days, a log fire burns in a
flagstone fireplace at one end of the room, and diners sometimes take
their hot drinks and sit on the hammered bronze and wood bench

before the hearth. Or they hunker down at the juice bar for a spell. Food here is straightforward and fresh. There are sandwiches, like smoked turkey with homemade mayonnaise, and a selection of Tex-Mex dishes, as well as salads and soup of the day. Follow your meal with a warm mug of the café's decaf brew, Common Ground, a blend of green tea, peppermint, and chicory. Lower Mills neighbors find fault with the Common Ground for closing on weekends and not serving liquor. "We need a real restaurant," they grouse. But the Common Ground is singular, and lovable just the way it is; if they want their weekends off, I can't really blame them. Attached to the café is the **Common Sense Wholesome Food Market** (2243 Dorchester Avenue, 617-298-5717), where you can get all the ingredients you'll need to cook up something healthy at home.

Xépa Café (657 Washington Street, 617-288-8770) is a Codman Square favorite for lunch, serving scrumptious food in very short order. Choose from the specials ($6.99), where fried chicken, oxtail, curried chicken, and stewed beef make daily appearances. Steamed fish and shrimp dinners go for a bit more. I like the curried chicken, cooked until it's just falling off the bone. Meals come with fried plantain, rice and beans, and a green salad. The dining room is sunny and pleasant and the tables have cut flowers, but don't think you have to dress up; this is a casual place. Chef-owner Paulincia Gattereau says she'll soon be adding homemade nonalcoholic tropical drinks to the menu. "Where do you think she learned to cook like this?" I asked my lunch mate. When we asked Paulincia, she shrugged, smiled and said, "Our mothers." Open Tuesday to Saturday (10:30 AM to 7 PM).

Glorified chicken, sautéed greens, sweet potato pie. Is it just me, or is **Bob the Chef's** (604 Columbus Avenue, 617-536-6204) culinary heaven for you, too? At night, the great soul food here is floated on the tunes of a laid-back jazz combo (Thursday to Saturday, from 7:30 PM; $2 cover). On Thursdays, Fridays, and Saturdays, the kitchen stays open until around midnight. Closed Mondays.

While it has something of a reputation as a vegetarian eatery, **Centre Street Café** (669A Centre Street, 617-524-9217) is not just a Kashiburger joint. There's no beef on the menu, but there is fowl. I like the chicken salad wrap, with big chunks of fresh free-range white meat tossed in a light lemon sauce. A house specialty, smoked bluefish cakes can be ordered as an appetizer or main. The setting is funky and the music good-timey.

A little storefront café near the Middlesex County Courthouse, **Sonya's** (89 Second Street, Cambridge, 617-661-1311), serves sandwiches on thick slices of freshly cut bread. There are a couple of soups on the hob, as well as hot specials like enchiladas, grilled chicken, and spicy peanut noodles. Sit at the counter, peer onto Second Street through a dozen windowpanes, and commune with the antique cod weather vanes. Visible from outside is a collection of antique children's kitchen appliances — yesteryear's Easy-Bake ovens.

While Harvard Square mutates around it, **Café Pamplona** (12 Bow Street) resists all change. Started nearly a half century ago by Pamplona native Josefina Yanguas, who continues to run it, this Cambridge institution is located in a whitewashed grotto under Cambridge Architectural Books. Pamplona's formula is simple: basic menu, crisp service, and the expectation that customers will stay as long as they please. The waiter will never say, "Are you still working on that?" Pamplona isn't trendy, nor is it dumpy. You won't see many undergrads here, though it's cheap enough. Pamplona attracts a slightly older professional crowd — professors and their paramours, perhaps. In short, it's a little trip to Europe. On the menu: empanadas (Spanish calzones in a cornmeal pastry), garlic soup, and filled baguettes delivered to your table with a jar of Dijon mustard. Finish with a parfait, a pastry, or chocolate mousse, and espresso.

Not far from Pamplona, diners crowd into **Mr. & Mrs. Bartley's** (1246 Massachusetts Avenue, Cambridge, 617-354-6559), sitting elbow to elbow at long tables for Bartley's famous fresh, juicy hamburgers. You can smell them grilling out on Mass Ave. I'm partial, however, to the turkey sandwich piled with stuffing, and topped with gravy and cranberry sauce. On hot days, stop by for a lime rickey. The ingredients are simple: fresh lime, soda water, crushed ice, and sugar. Bartley's makes them better than anyone in town.

SECRET
CANDLEPINS

Candlepin bowling is a variation of the alley game that involves tall, slender "candles" rather than curvy clubs, and a pint-sized ball instead of a boulder. Everything else is pretty much as you might expect at any bowling alley: the fumigated shoes, the burnished lanes, the clatter of spares and strikes — but fewer of the latter. It's said that a perfect, all strikes game has never been bowled in candlepins.

Most of the big alleys have both 10-pin and candlepin lanes. But for candlepin purists, two places stand out. Opened in 1939, the 15-lane **Sacco's Bowl-Haven** (45 Day Street, Somerville, 617-776-0552) still has the original maple alleys and is now run by a fourth generation of Saccos. Every Friday night (9 PM to midnight), things get just a little weirder when "Midnight Bowling" begins. Lights are dimmed and cartoons from the 1930s to '50s are screened on the walls to the entertainment of punters and mild consternation of serious bowlers. If the bowling gets stale, you can try billiards and pool ($7.50 per hour). Open Sundays and Mondays (until 11:30 PM), and Tuesday to Friday (until midnight). The cost is $2 per string, or you can get an hourly package that includes that spiffy pair of shoes.

Part lounge, part lanes, the **Milky Way Lounge & Lanes** (403–405 Centre Street, 617-524-3740) is a quaint four-lane candlepin alley that attracts trendy-somethings and young families. The Milky Way is festooned with homegrown décor, with 1950s lampshades (faux leopard skin, contiki prints) and Christmas lights glittering in the lanes' polished surfaces. The bowling alley is of the same vintage as Sacco's, but these are not the sweetest conditions. Diehard candlepin bowlers go elsewhere. In a stroke of genius, when half of the alleys were closed down to make room for the lounge, builders put up picture windows. If you walk down past the bar toward the waitress stand, you can look in on the 70-year-old machinery that runs the remaining four lanes, with candlepins nesting and ready for the next round. The Milky Way is also a cool nightclub with live local bands and dancing. A couple of pool tables and a new table hockey game round out the social pleasures of this JP classic. You can order food (pizzas, pasta, salads; $12 to $18) from the upstairs café, **Bella Luna** (405 Centre Street, Jamaica Plain, 617-524-6060). In short, the Milky Way is a great combination of all you need in life — food, beer, entertainment, friends, and candlepins.

SECRET
CANDY FACTORY

You know those pastel, heart-shaped candies with "HUG ME," "BE TRUE," and "MY GIRL" printed on them in fuzzy red ink? Made in Boston (the Cambridge part). Sweethearts are one of a handful of candies manufactured by NECCO, the **New England Confectionery Company**.

The origins of this candy-coated New England manufacturing mainstay date back to 1847, when Boston confectioner Oliver Chase invented the first American candy machine, the Lozenge Cutter, and what would later be called the NECCO wafer was born. The candy industry picked up steam as the Industrial Revolution got underway during the 19th century. At the turn of the 20th century, NECCO was born in the merger of Oliver Chase's old firm and two other candy companies. They set up shop in a new plant at Summer and Melcher streets, South Boston; you can still walk along Necco Street in Southie. In 1927, NECCO moved to its present plant in East Cambridge — the largest space in the world devoted to the manufacturing of sweets. Also, look for the candy-striped tower atop 254 Mass Avenue, another NECCO property.

NECCO still makes its famous hearts and wafers in its East Cambridge factory, where an unmistakable sugary odor often fills the air. The company also manufactures and distributes Mary Janes, Sky Bars, Thin Mints, Mighty Malts, and Clark bars. To the eternal consternation of many (including yours truly), NECCO does not offer factory tours. Somewhat consolingly, there is a **factory outlet store** (134 Cambridge Street, at First Street, Cambridge) across from the Lechmere T station.

As you walk along the side of the plant, note the industrial-sized nozzles for loading raw materials: "corn syrup," "sugar syrup," and "coating." Then go inside and fill your basket with bulk or boxed candies you'd have a hard time finding anywhere else. Open weekdays (9 AM to 4 PM).

Romantics can get their very own, very short sayings printed on Sweethearts, with caveats. Your message is subject to company approval, and you have to purchase an entire "print run" of 3,500 pounds of candies. (Also, you're not going to write a sonnet on a candy lozenge the size of a fingernail.) As an alternative, if you think you have a winning idea for a Sweetheart saying, write to King of Hearts, NECCO, 134 Cambridge Street, Cambridge, MA 02141. If you're lucky, they'll steal your idea.

And another thing: My esteemed *Secret Chicago* colleague notes that NECCO wafers can be used to cheat the Illinois toll booths. I'm not recommending you try this when you visit the Land of Lincoln; I just thought you should know.

SECRET

CEMETERIES

On a scorching August afternoon just beyond the screen of tall trees that cloak **Forest Hills Cemetery** (95 Forest Hills Avenue, Jamaica Plain, 617-524-0128), city life was buzzing. But here in this rural burying ground of 99,000 souls, nothing stirred but a gaggle of Canada geese grazing among the headstones. Forest Hills, founded in 1848, is the tranquil permanent residence of a host of notables, including poets e.e. cummings and Anne Sexton, athlete Reggie Lewis, writer Ezra Pound, playwright Eugene O'Neill, and abolitionist William Lloyd Garrison. More than a burying ground, Forest Hills is also a wildlife sanctuary and botanical garden, as well as an al fresco museum of Victorian sculpture, where angels and obelisks are set in a backdrop of ancient trees and bubbly outcrops of Roxbury pudding-stone. The cemetery sponsors events ranging from art installations to public lectures and tours of the grounds. It's fine, however, to keep your ambitions modest here on this hallowed ground, and stroll or drive around on your own (dawn to dusk); free. In the office, you can buy a guidebook, as well as maps and brochures on areas of interest, birds, and temporary art installations.

"We can find no better spot," said the *Boston Courier* at the 1831 dedication of Mt. Auburn Cemetery, "for the rambles of curiosity, health or pleasure; none sweeter, for the whispers of affection among the living; none lovelier, for the last rest of our kindred." The elder sister of Forest Hills, **Mt. Auburn Cemetery** (Friends of Mt. Auburn Cemetery, 580 Mt. Auburn Road, 617-864-9646) is another of Greater Boston's rich natural areas. Here, too, you can look for memorials to the famous dead. Charles Bulfinch, Winslow Homer, Henry Wadsworth Longfellow, Oliver Wendell Holmes, Mary Baker Eddy, Isabella Stewart Gardner, Buckminster Fuller, and B.F. Skinner are all buried here.

Like Forest Hills, Mt. Auburn goes far beyond its fundamental task of perpetuating the memory of the dead. One of America's great landscape parks, the cemetery is an arboretum of fantastic scope and vintage, with more than 5,000 trees of 700 varieties. The largest of Mt. Auburn's trees are the black oaks and European beeches, with trunks up to three feet in diameter. Mt. Auburn is also a botanical garden alive with blooms from March crocuses to November

chrysanthemums, a gallery of sculpture, a wildlife sanctuary, and a favorite haunt for birds (see "Secret Birds"). A one-hour audiocassette driving tour of the grounds is available for rent (during office hours, 8:30 AM to 3:30 PM, daily) or for purchase from the Friends of Mt. Auburn Cemetery (phone above).

On a much smaller scale, but no less fascinating, are Boston's ancient graveyards. As well as being the resting places of patriots and pirates, the burying grounds are of interest for their headstones and markers carved with death's heads and cherubs, and sometimes adorned with cryptic verses and indifferent spelling ("Here Lyes the Mortal Parte"). Of Boston's four Puritan-era burying grounds, **Copp's Hill Burying Ground** (Hull and Snowhill streets, off Salem Street), established in 1659, has the prettiest setting. On a rise above the harbor, this peaceful spot is home to a host of colonial cadavers, including Cotton and Increase Mather, as well as many freed slaves who made their home in the early North End. Buried here, too, is Robert Newton, the sexton of the **Old North Church** who was responsible for getting Paul Revere off on the right foot (see "Secret Midnight Ride"). In the same year, those pesky redcoats used the old burying ground for target practice; you can see the lasting effects of this insult to the emerging nation on several pockmarked headstones.

A couple of Copp's Hill asides: Across from the burying ground is an odd little clapboard house at 44 Hull Street, wedged between brick-clad townhouses. The little house's front door faces a tight alley, while the side along the street shows the depth of the house to be a mere 10 feet, making it the **narrowest house in Boston**. It's a private residence. Also, the **Great Molasses Spill** of 1919 occurred near here when a 2.5-million-gallon tank of molasses, used in the making of rum, exploded. Twenty-one people were killed in the ensuing 12-foot wave. It's said the town smelled of molasses for decades after.

King's Chapel Burying Ground (adjacent to King's Chapel, 58 Tremont Street), founded in 1630, has the distinction of being Boston's first cemetery. It's home to the graves of John Winthrop, first governor of the Massachusetts Bay Colony, and William Dawes, the *other* guy who rode out to Concord to warn the Minutemen that the British were coming. The letter "A" on the headstone of Elizabeth Pain is said to have inspired Hawthorne's novel *The Scarlet Letter*. Also along Tremont Street, the **Old Granary Burying Ground** (next to Park Street Church, Park and Tremont streets), founded in 1660, contains the graves of five victims of the Boston Massacre, as well as those of Samuel Adams and Paul Revere. But many people who visit come to pay tribute to Elizabeth Foster Goose (or Vergoose), said to be the original Mother Goose of nursery rhyme fame. Finally, the **Central Burying Ground**, founded in 1756, is located in the southwest corner of Boston Common. Here you'll find the graves of a number of Revolutionary War soldiers, as well as the portrait artist Gilbert Stuart (1755–1828), best known for his painting of the head of George Washington that graces our quarter.

There are many lesser-known but no less venerable burying grounds in other parts of the city. The **Dorchester North Burying Ground** (Columbia Road and Stoughton Street), dedicated in 1633, and Roxbury's **Eliot Burying Ground** (Eustis and Washington streets), established in 1630, are as old as the downtown graveyards, but much less visited. In addition to those named here, the city of Boston maintains nine other 17th-, 18th-, and 19th-century burying grounds (www.cityofboston.gov/parks/buryinggrounds/about.asp). West of the city, many of Boston's famous 19th-century literary figures lie in eternal rest at "the Westminster Abbey of America," **Sleepy Hollow Cemetery** (Court Lane, Concord). Most of the members of the Alcott family, including Louisa May, are buried here. Look also for the graves of Nathaniel Hawthorne, Henry David Thoreau and family, and Ralph Waldo Emerson, as well as those of Daniel Chester French and Elizabeth Peabody.

In what might be termed a "death styles of the rich and famous" show, the annual **Tour de Graves** (Historic Burying Ground Initiative, contact Kelly Thomas, 617-635-4505, ext. 6516, kthomas@ci.boston. ma.us) takes the stout of heart and limb on a 20-mile guided bike trek of Boston's burying grounds and garden cemeteries each October. Call for details and pre-registration (required). Register early because it does sell out. The fee is usually about $10 and includes a guidebook and picnic lunch. A souvenir T-shirt runs $10 or so.

SECRET

CHARLES RIVER

London has the Thames. Paris has the Seine. Boston has its Charles River. So pervasive is the influence on Boston of this leisurely body of water that you can hardly escape communing with it. Take the Red Line to or from Cambridge over the Longfellow, or "Salt and Pepper," Bridge (so called because its towers resemble condiment shakers) and enjoy one of the city's best river views. Walk along the Charles River Esplanade or enjoy Memorial Drive's car-free zone on a summer weekend afternoon. Thanks to the Big Dig, revel in the glorious span of the Leonard P. Zakim Bunker Hill Memorial Bridge. But to really get to know the Charles and its denizens, you have to "shove off."

At home in the wide Charles River Basin, **Community Boating** (21 David Mugar Way, near the Hatch Shell, 617-523-1038) offers blissful river sailing, canoeing, kayaking, and windsurfing. They welcome people at all skill levels, from beginners to seasoned water bugs, from April through the chilly winds of October, weekdays (1 PM to sunset) and weekends (9 AM to sunset). There is a two-day membership available ($50) for those who already know how to sail. For the rest, memberships start at $75 for a 45-day period, which includes all the sailing and instruction you need.

Upriver at the **Charles River Canoe and Kayak Center** (Route 30, Newton, 617-965-5110; and Christian Herter Park, off Soldier's Field Road, 617-462-2513), you can rent watercraft: canoes, kayaks, or — if you're content like Ratty and Mole with "messing about" — a jaunty rowboat. The Newton location is open Monday to Friday (10 AM to 6 PM), and weekends (9 AM to 6 PM), while the Boston boathouse is open Fridays (1 PM to dusk) and weekends (10 AM to dusk). Both are open from May to October.

Those who have their own boats can contact the **Metropolitan District Commission** (617-727-9547, www.state.ma.us/mdc/charlesr.htm) for a list of small boat launches and paddling conditions on the Charles. The MDC doesn't recommend that novices canoe or kayak downstream of the Boston University Bridge because of swift currents. Also, this area is not the best for quiet water boating because of motorboat traffic, but you do get a great view of the city skyline from the area of the BU Bridge. Experienced paddlers can continue under the bridge on into the Basin, and even negotiate the locks at Charles River Dam to the harbor.

One of Boston's most beloved annual sporting events is the **Head of the Charles Regatta** (www.hocr.org), which takes place during the third week of October. This international rowing meet attracts hundreds of competitors, who race three miles from the Boston University Boathouse to Christian Herter Park. It's the largest single-day rowing event in the world. The best viewing is on the Harvard Square section of Memorial Drive. If the sight of so many sculls inspires you, sign up for rowing instruction. Courses in sweep (one oar per rower) or sculling (two oars per rower) are offered at **Community Rowing** (Daly Rink, Nonantum Road, Brighton/ Newton, 617-964-2455) from April to October.

Those who would rather leave the river navigation to the experts have a wealth of choices. **Boston Duck Tours** (617-723-3825) whisks passengers around the city in vintage World War II amphibious vehicles. Just when everyone on board is thinking that nothing could be finer than driving down Newbury Street in a bright orange tank, the "conducktor" drives straight into the Charles River. The adventure continues as the tank–boat tools up the Charles, where anyone with the urge can take a turn behind the wheel. The tours run from April to November, and sell out quickly in summer. You can buy tickets up to two days in advance from booths in the Prudential Center and outside the *New England Aquarium*.

Offering cruises along the Charles River, **Charles Riverboat Company** (100 CambridgeSide Place, Cambridge, 617-621-3001) vessels depart from the CambridgeSide Galleria mall for 55-minute tours daily from June to August (10:30 AM to 5 PM), and on weekends in April, May, and September. Also from the Galleria, take a spin on a Venetian gondola (see "Secret Gondolas").

SECRET

CHINATOWN

History has a way of piling up in Chinatown. You can still peer down **Ping On Alley** (off Essex Street between Oxford and Edinboro streets), "the street of peace and security," where Boston's first Chinese immigrants, arriving to help lay the first telephone lines, pitched tents and built communal cooking ovens in 1875. By 1890, the area between Kneeland and Essex streets was a full-fledged Chinese "colony," boasting the city's first Chinese restaurant, Hong Far Low, at 36 1/2 Harrison Avenue. These days, Chinatown is home to many Asian groups, especially Vietnamese and Cambodians, who began arriving in the 1970s.

Mirroring the growth of Boston's Asian community, Chinatown has begun to sprout beyond its traditional borders between Washington and Hudson streets and along Essex, Beach, and Kneeland streets. In the process, it has transformed the so-called Combat Zone along Washington Street (once known for its strip joints and pornography shops) into a street of eateries. **Penang** (685 Washington Street, 617-451-6373), part of a New York chain, has put some serious thought into its decor, creating a tropical jungle lodge look. The Malaysian cuisine is equally intriguing, relying on a blend of Chinese, Middle Eastern, Thai, and Indian cooking techniques. Recommended: The yam pot, an edible taro bowl stuffed with meat and vegetables. It comes with chicken ($9.95) or seafood ($11.95) and subtle sauces. Fire-eating patrons won't be at all disappointed in the spicy dishes.

Ever since Vietnamese began arriving in large numbers, the noodle shop has been the staple of Chinatown dining. There are scores of places, in Chinatown and elsewhere in the city (Dorchester Avenue and Fields Corner are prime spots), where you can walk in and order a hearty bowl of pho. Taking the concept to the next level, **Pho Pasteur** (682 Washington Street, 617-482-7467) provides a pleasant ambience (lighting, fresh flowers) in addition to yummy food. The chain has branches in Allston (137 Brighton Avenue, Allston, 617-783-2340), Harvard Square (36 Dunster Street, Cambridge, 617-864-4100), and Boston (119 Newbury Street, 617-262-8200; and 123 Stuart Street, 617-742-2436).

Those short on time patronize the **Food Court** (46 Beach Street, second floor), with its six stalls selling fast Asian fare from all over the Orient. It's a good place to try something different, such as Creamsicle-colored Thai iced tea or iced coffee with "pearls" (chewy balls of tapioca).

There are dozens of other restaurants to choose from in Chinatown, many of them open into the wee hours of the morning. **Chau Chow** (45 Beach Street, 617-426-6266), **Dynasty** (33 Edinboro Street, 617-350-7777), and **East Ocean City** (617-542-2504), are all quality places, open past 2 AM, so there's no reason to resort to IHOP.

While many people come to Chinatown to sample the cooking of Thailand, Cambodia, Vietnam, Malaysia, and the Chinese regions of Canton and Sichuan, the majority come to shop for produce, baked goods, meats, pharmaceuticals, and, yes, goldfish. Not far from the **China Gate** (Beach and Hudson streets), official entrance to Chinatown, **Hing Shing Pastry** (67 Beach Street, 617-451-1162) offers sweet proof that Chinese desserts go well beyond the restaurant fortune cookie. On a warm day, the aroma of almonds, coconut, and honey drifts into Beach Street. Inside the tiny shop, glass cases are stacked high with glazed moon cakes, stamped with red Chinese characters and filled with lotus seed paste. There are almond cookies, coconut cakes, chewy deep-fried bean-paste donuts sprinkled with sesame seeds, and steamed sponge cakes. Savory baked and steamed items make an appearance, too: chicken dumplings the size of a lotus flower are an excellent light lunch. And you can't beat the price (60 cents). Or sample the baked buns stuffed with ham or beef curry. Everything is fresh here; you can make sure by watching a batch of hot buns travel from kitchen to counter. If the Hing Shing is too crowded, try the **Ho Yuen Bakery** (54 Beach Street, 617-426-8320) just up the street.

On Chinatown's diminutive scale, **Mei Tung Oriental Food Super Market** (109 Lincoln Street, 617-426-1917) is vast. This multi-aisle food store, pharmacy, and kitchen supply depot stocks everything from quail eggs to bamboo back-scratchers. The herbalist sells the usual range of Far Eastern cures, as well as lottery tickets — should good health escape you, perhaps good fortune won't. At the back of the store, the wheels of commerce are in plain view with men unloading produce from trucks, butchers hacking and packing meats and fishes, and women sorting boxes of greens for the market.

When speaking of Asian groceries, I can't omit **Dot Ave** (Dorchester Avenue), where a linear Little Saigon has sprung up over the last decade. Along this main Dorchester drag are several large Vietnamese grocery stores, small restaurants, and diminutive "donut" shops. The latter, such as **Anna's Donuts** (1035 Dorchester Avenue, 617-436-5652) sell Asian savories (steamed meat buns) and Vietnamese coffee (an aromatic brew served with sweetened condensed milk), as well as some American-style pastries.

Back in Chinatown, **Nam Buk Hong Chinese Herbs** (75 Harrison Avenue, 617-426-8227) is one of those magical doorways into another world. Today, a middle-aged couple is having a prescription filled.

The couple watches as the herbalist crushes, grinds, and pulverizes a half dozen powders and unguents, weighs them out in a brass balance, then empties the entire concoction onto crisp brown paper laid out on the old oak counter. The order complete, the herbalist goes to a wooden abacus and fills the shop with a clacking of calculations. If you're just looking, keep an eye out for "gift packs" of exotic dried mushrooms, essences of chicken, boxes of ginseng tea, bits of ginkgo, crocodile bile ("for asthma"), reindeer antlers, and dried seahorses.

Shopping for gifts in Chinatown is much more inspiring than a trip to the mall. A fashion designer in Vietnam for 25 years before coming to Boston to set up shop in Chinatown, Kim Pham now runs the tiny **Kim Fashion Design** (12 Kneeland Street, 617-426-5740). The shop is filled with her creations: satin mandarin jackets with hand-made clasps, velvet accessories, slinky silk dresses, hand-embroidered fabrics, and flowing scarves. At **Oriental Fortune Giftland** (95–97 Chauncy Street, 617-350-6132), shop for embroidered pajamas, coolie hats, carved cork landscapes, paper lanterns, glass figurines, plastic ninja swords, cocktail umbrellas, incense, and black gongfu slippers. Then dive down into **Aqua World** (20 Tyler Street, 617-426-2227), where dozens of varieties of gauzy goldfish swim in 40-gallon tanks in a cave-like shop, quiet but for the gurgling of aerators.

The **International Society** (276 Tremont Street, 617-542-4599) exhibits works by Asian artists and members of many of Boston's other ethnic communities. As well as sponsoring concerts and craft workshops, it has four resident theater companies and a resident dance company.

SECRET
CHOCOLATE

The production of chocolate arrived in America when an entrepreneur named John Hanau brought cocoa beans to Boston from the West Indies. His partner in the enterprise was James Baker, who opened a processing house in Dorchester Lower Mills. Yes, Dorchester is the North American birthplace of hot chocolate.

Today, still licked by the green Neponset River, Baker's handsome Victorian chocolate mill has been converted to moderately priced lofts and dubbed **Baker's Chocolate Apartments** (1200 Adams Street). One half expects gingerbread people to come marching out. Several other brick and cedar-shingle factory buildings cluster along the river's edge, including one that's been turned into upscale condos, and another — the neo-Classical administration building of the Baker Chocolate Factory — that will house subsidized artists' studios and a gallery. Meanwhile, a stroll around the neighborhood will turn up a few antiques shops (see "Secret Salvage" and "Secret 20th-Century Artifacts"), as well one of the most unusual cafés in the city, the **Common Ground Café** (see "Secret Cafés"). Otherwise, Lower Mills' main drag is composed of the usual charming assortment of Dorchester commercial interests — a barber shop, the Curl Up and Dye Salon, and a couple of pubs featuring New England Boiled Dinner.

So much for the history of chocolate. Time for a snack. I visited the newish LA **Burdick** (52 Brattle Street, Cambridge, 617-491-4340) with a soupçon of doubt. Could Burdick's hot chocolate be as good as Angelina's, the turn-of-the-century café in Paris where I'd enjoyed

so many chocolate afternoons? Yep. Rich, intense, and thick,
Burdick's hot chocolate is a drug. Try it at your peril. Patrons at this
chocolate den, unmindful of the clattering kitchen, sit at tiny tables
topped with craft paper. They (all women; do men come here?) sip in
pairs and singly from white bowls of hot chocolate and nibble on
tarts. As for the candies, they're handmade (in New Hampshire) and
sold at $12 a pound. Buy them as gifts all done up in craft paper and
wooden boxes, closed with a satin ribbon and gold sealing wax.
Choose from among solid ingots, assortments of bonbons, and boxed
sets of the company's adorable chocolate mice or penguins.

One of the great pleasures of living in Boston is walking into
Rosie's Bakery and saying, "I'll have a chocolate orgasm, please. No,
make that two. Thanks. Have a nice day." Look for these fudge-iced
chocolate chip brownies from weight-watchers hell at Rosie's various
locations (South station, 617-439-4684; 9 Boylston Street, Brookline,
617-277-5629; and 243 Hampshire Street, Cambridge, 617-354-1843).
Besides Rosie's, another downtown choco-thing is the mocha chip
cookie at **Rebecca's** (500 Boylston Street, 617-536-5900, and a dozen
other downtown and suburban locations). It's big, it's challenging,
and it's chocolate. Wash it down with a bodacious espresso.

No self-respecting dessert menu would be caught without at least one
chocolate confection. The best chocolate blitzes I've encountered are
at **Lucca** (226 Hanover Street, 617-742-9200), where the flourless
chocolate cake will make you cry "uncle!" In Cambridge, **Sandrine's**
(8 Holyoke Street, Cambridge, 617-497-5300) chocolate kügelhopf is
another killer — drizzled with warm chocolate ganache and caramel,
and topped with vanilla ice cream.

Chocolate gets all over everything during weekends in February and
March, when Old Town Trolley does its narrated, three-hour
Chocolate Tour (617-269-7150). Patrons satisfy the urge at the Top

of the Hub, 52 floors above Boston, with a to-be-announced chocolate dessert; at the Hampshire House, with a bowl of roasted maple walnut chocolate soup; and at Le Meridien Hotel, where they dig into the chocolate buffet. The price is $50 per person.

SECRET

CHRISTIAN SCIENCE

The **Christian Science Center** complex in Boston's Back Bay has been almost famous for years for a quirky and wonderful attraction called the **Mapparium** (Christian Science Center, 1 Norway Street, at Massachusetts Avenue, 617-450-2000). This 30-foot, walk-through, stained-glass globe is set in a bronze framework and lit from within by hundreds of lights. You enter via a bridge, finding yourself in the center of the earth — but not quite *this* earth. Built in 1934, the globe's contours are frozen in pre-World War II political divisions. Look in vain for newfangled countries like Israel or Vietnam. The globe's acoustics are distinctive, too. Because glass doesn't absorb sound, anyone whispering in, say, Madagascar can be heard clearly way over in Chile. Closed during 2001 for renovation, the Mapparium will reopen along with its new sound and light program when the new Mary Baker Eddy Library (below) is unveiled in autumn 2002.

Outside on the 14-acre Christian Science Center concourse is the 1894 Romanesque Mother Church, with its 1906 domed Renaissance-Byzantine extension. The church anchors one end of the I.M. Pei-designed concourse, where a reflecting pool, flanked by high- and low-rise church administration buildings, ends in a colossal fountain.

There are half-hour tours of the Mother Church (617-450-3790) Monday to Saturday (10 AM to 4 PM), and Sundays (11:15 AM to 3 PM); free.

The founder of the Church of Christ Scientist was Mary Baker Eddy (1821–1910), a charismatic figure not well understood by those outside of her followers. A couple of new developments should bring this influential New England woman into the light. At the Christian Science Center, a new 81,000-square-foot library devoted to Eddy is slated to open in fall 2002. It will house Mrs. Baker's voluminous correspondence and papers, as well as the papers of a number of other historical figures, such as Theodore Roosevelt, Susan B. Anthony, Bronson Alcott, and Henry Wadsworth Longfellow. The museum will also include New England artifacts and photos, as well as interactive exhibits exploring the basis of Mrs. Eddy's teaching, the link between spirituality and health.

Nearing completion at the time of research was yet another paean to Mrs. Eddy. The **Longyear Museum** (1125 Boylston Street, Route 9, Chestnut Hill, 617-278-9000) is a 25,000-square-foot museum housing a large collection of Eddy memorabilia. Though it is a biographical museum, Mrs. Eddy herself warned against the "cult of personality," so the museum devotes itself not to worship, but to study and reflection on the life, times, and associates of Mrs. Eddy. There is a bookshop and research library (open to the public), and by the time the museum opens officially, there will be a small cafeteria and outdoor dining terrace. It's a beautiful space; one might pay the admission fee just to pass an afternoon enjoying its curvaceous halls and comfortable sitting areas.

SECRET
CIRCUS

It was supposed to be just another workday. Visit a circus school. Take some notes. Get home in time for dinner. But before I could mouth an excuse, I was climbing the ladder.

I'm listening to the instructions of the women surrounding me on the 30-foot-high platform. One of them says, "Now, I want you to reach out and take the bar." So I lean out over the net and circle my hands around the wobbling trapeze. Tito calls from below, "Move your hands a little further apart. That's it." I rest my weight on one of the women's knees, point my legs out into the air, and, with a "Hup!" from Tito, I'm flying.

Enjoying a banner first season in Boston, **Tito Gaona Flying Trapeze and Fantasy Circus** (contact Judy Barstow, 617-262-5839, [mailing address: 401 Commonwealth Avenue, Boston MA 02215]; or Tito Gaona, 941-412-9305, TitoGaona@aol.com, www.townonline. koz.com/visit/titogaona) was set up on the expansive lawn of Cedar Hill Camp in Waltham. It was a beautiful mid-summer evening, the horizon laced with purple clouds. A little crowd sat on the sunburned grass, watching this group of adults learn something about the art of flying.

And I am flying! "Kick back! Forward!" calls Tito. "Look at your toes!"

The net swings past below me, the sky reels over my head. After the initial back and forth, my momentum slows. Then, things get interesting. With Tito coaching from the ground, I discover how to power up with the backswing by throwing my legs forward. But it's the upswing I really like. Here I get to look at my toes. I find those toes reassuring out here.

Finally, Tito senses I'm tiring. (Maybe it's because I'm saying "ooohaouaooh.") My hands have had it. "On the next swing, I want you to just fall on your back," calls Tito. Gladly. Out go my legs in front of me and my hands let go of their own accord as if to say, well, it's about time. It's a bumpy landing, but here I am. I lie there on the bobbing net, spread-eagled. Tito walks under the net and looks up at me. "How're you feeling?" Oh fine. Then he must have given me a pep talk, but I can't be sure. I was busy thinking, "I'm alive. I'm alive. I'm a little nauseous. But I'm alive."

"Come on down," says Tito. "Hey, she's been drinking too much tequila!" he teases as I careen around the net trying to get a foothold. The shakiness, says Tito when my feet find the earth, is from the adrenaline. "The first time you feel it, you're not used to it. You don't know what to do with it," he says. And a student laughs, adding, "Then you get used to it. Then you get addicted to it!"

"Okay," says Tito, "next time, you'll go without sitting on the lap." Next time?

Most of the students here have some background in movement. There's a dancer, a cheerleading coach, a gymnast. But you don't have to be an athlete (take me for example). And students come from all walks of life. Says one, "People probably think only a bunch of weirdoes would spend their spare time on a flying trapeze. But we're very normal. I'm getting my MBA at Harvard; there's a stockbroker, a schoolteacher. We're just average people."

Every flight is followed by one of Tito's private pep talks. I can hear him going over the "trick" with a student — the good, the not so good, and ways to fix it. "Not so good on the pike," says Tito. "But you've got beautiful phoooom!" he adds, slicing the air with his hands. It's too bad I missed my pep talk. I'm pretty sure I didn't have phoooom. But then, I'm just getting started.

Tito, a member of the Flying Gaonas, has been flying with circuses, including the Big Apple Circus and Ringling Brothers' Barnum & Bailey, since he was in grade school. Beginning in 2002, the circus school will have a permanent indoor arena in Boston's metro west region. Call or visit the Web site for an update.

Tito's is the only trapeze class in town. But if you just want to learn how to juggle, check out "the oldest drop-in juggling club in continuous operation in the world." It's the MIT **Juggling Club** (contact Arthur Lewbel, 781-862-3089, lewbel@bc.edu), which meets on the MIT campus every Sunday, year round (3:30 PM to 6:30 PM). All are welcome. Call for details on the meeting place, as it changes seasonally. If you want to get a head start, go first to the **Harvard Juggling Club** (Joey Cousin, 617-493-3310, jcousin@fas.harvard.edu), which meets Sundays (2 PM to 3:30 PM), with similar high jinks.

SECRET
CITY VIEWS

Some lament its closing, but the Back Bay's John Hancock Observatory was not the only, nor even the best, place to see Boston whole. Scaling another Back Bay edifice to the 52-story **Prudential Center Skywalk** (800 Boylston Street, 617-859-0648) has always had a slight edge over the Hancock trip because you don't have the unlovely Pru in your view. Open Monday to Saturday (10 AM to

10 PM), and Sundays (noon to 10 PM); $4. Call first to make sure the observatory is open.

There's no charge at all to mount the **Bunker Hill Monument** (Monument Square, 617-242-5641), where the views of the harbor and skyline are superb. The catch is that you have to walk up a spiral of 294 stone steps. It's good for you. Stick around for one of the exciting ranger talks on this pivotal revolutionary battle, then wander around Charlestown's charming gaslight district — like Beacon Hill without the frosting. Open daily (9 AM to 5 PM). A state holiday, **Bunker Hill Day** (June 17), celebrates the Battle of Bunker Hill.

Free *and* sporting a whizzy elevator, Marriott's **Custom House Tower** (State and India streets, 617-310-6300) practically tips you right into the blue harbor. With its glorious vantage point and open observation deck, this is the best of these three aeries. There is history here, too. In 1915, when the original Greek Revival building was topped with the 495-foot Classical Revival tower, the Custom House was the tallest building in Boston. At the time, the city had a 125-foot height restriction, but being a federal property, the Custom House ignored the rule, giving dismayed Bostonians their first skyscraper. Now that the building is an extended-stay hotel, trips to the top are by guided expedition only, Sunday to Friday (10 AM and 4 PM), and Saturdays (4 PM only). During other times, the entrance lobby with its lofty rotunda is worth a look. On the mezzanine level, you'll find maritime artifacts on loan from Salem's Peabody Essex Museum. Be sure to call the Marriott Custom House Tower in advance of your visit, as the tours were suspended for reasons of security — either temporarily or permanently — at press time.

Moving south, surmount South Boston's **Dorchester Heights** (Thomas Park, off G Street, Boston National Historical Park, 617-242-5642), where colonial forces mustered in March 1776, dragging artillery from Fort Ticonderoga to lay siege to the redcoats across the bay in Boston proper. Commemorating the colonists' March 17 victory here, still celebrated in Massachusetts as Evacuation Day, is a 215-foot white marble **tower** with a spectacular vista of Boston and Dorchester Bay. Open July and August, Saturdays and Sundays (10 AM to 4 PM), Wednesdays (4 PM to 8 PM); free. To get there, follow Dorchester Street (not Avenue) to Telegraph Street.

Some quick picks: In the North End, **Copp's Hill Burying Ground** (see "Secret Cemeteries") rises above the harbor with views of the Leonard P. Zakim Bunker Hill Memorial Bridge. Diners at the **Museum of Science Skyline Room** (Science Park, Monsignor O'Brien Highway, 617-723-2500) look out at eye level across the Charles River Basin and Beacon Hill. One of the best places to photograph or just gaze at the Boston skyline at sunset is the **Boston University Bridge**, which crosses the Charles just before the river bends northward. Still further out, the **Concord Turnpike**, known more prosaically as Route 2, has a big-picture view of the skyline at the eastbound Arlington Heights exit.

SECRET
CLASSICAL

"On any given night," writes local scholar Sam Bass Warner, Jr. in *Greater Boston*, "the Boston city region sends more musical sounds toward the heavens than any other American place except such giants as New York, Chicago and Los Angeles." And, of these infinite sounds, classical music is undoubtedly the Hub's forte.

Besides, we got there first. Boston can boast the country's oldest symphony orchestra, the **Boston Symphony Orchestra** (BSO). Founded in 1881, in its first year the fledgling symphony performed 20 concerts to a total audience of around 85,000. Today, under the baton of Seiji Ozawa, the BSO's yearly audience is one and a half million, and concerts number 250 annually. The home of the BSO is **Symphony Hall** (301 Massachusetts Avenue, 617-266-1492, box office 617-266-1200), which is also no spring chicken, having recently celebrated its centenary. Sitting toad-like at the corner of Mass Ave and Huntington Avenue, the Hall's brick-box design may not look like much from the outside, but the interior is said to be not only acoustically perfect, but *more* perfect than any other concert hall in the world. Now how do we know that? In the 1960s, acoustic scientist Leo Beranek decided he was going to find the world's finest concert hall. He considered more than 50 halls all over the world, and our Symphony Hall came out on top. Of course, the fact that Leo was a member of the BSO board of trustees played no role in the decision. A commemorative plaque for Beranek hangs in the celebrated building's hallway, as does a memorial to the *Titanic* musicians who "went down playing."

During the summer months, the BSO escapes to Tanglewood in the Berkshire Mountains of western Massachusetts, leaving the great hall to the **Boston Pops** (same phone) under the direction of Keith Lockhart.

Well before the BSO was created, a group of German musicians formed Boston's **Handel and Haydn Society** (box office, 617-266-3605). The year was 1815, and three years later the group made further history by presenting the American premiere of Handel's *Messiah*. The group continues to perform the works of H&H on period instruments, as well as a smattering of Bach, Beethoven, and others.

It also does an annual jazz concert. Other early music groups include
Boston Baroque (box office, 617-484-9200) and **Boston Cecelia**
(box office, 617-232-4540), one of the city's most respected choral
groups. The **Boston Early Music Festival** (box office, 617-661-
1812) brings the works of primordial composers to performance
spaces across the city every other June, along with exhibitions and a
full-scale dress performance of a Baroque opera.

Like fans of minor league baseball, classical music lovers often find a
home with Boston's smaller, perhaps zestier, ensembles. The **Boston
Philharmonic** (box office, 617-868-6696) performs under the baton
of the predictably wild-haired Benjamin Zander. Performances take
place on Saturday nights at the New England Conservatory's Jordan
Hall (30 Gainsborough Street) and Sunday afternoons at Harvard's
Sanders Theatre (45 Quincy Street, Cambridge) from October to April.
Zander gives a lecture before each performance. Taking classical
music to the streets, the new **Boston Landmarks Orchestra** (617-
520-2200), under the direction of Charles Ansbacher, celebrates "the
significance between site and sound" with venue-hopping summer
concerts at Boston Common, Franklin Park, and Jamaica Pond, and
on George's Island. All performances are free.

Site and setting are also a large part of the appeal of a host of high-
quality concert series at smaller venues. The stately **Shirley-Eustis
House** (33 Shirley Street, 617-442-2275) holds Sunday afternoon
recitals each spring and fall. The birthplace of Unitarianism (1776),
King's Chapel (School and Tremont streets, 617-227-2155), hosts
early music concerts with an occasional jazz set each Tuesday (12:15
PM); $2. **Trinity Church** (206 Clarendon Street, 617-536-0944)
sponsors free half-hour organ concerts each Friday (12:15 PM) from
mid-September to June on its 6,898-pipe organ, featuring organists
from the world over. The **Isabella Stewart Gardner Museum**

(2 Palace Road, 617-734-1359) has Saturday and Sunday afternoon chamber music (1:30 PM) in the Tapestry Room from September to April. The price of the concert ($17) includes admission to museum. The **Museum of Fine Arts** (465 Huntington Avenue, 617-267-9300) offers al fresco "concerts in the courtyard" during the summer and other musical events throughout the year, featuring the resident early music trio and many guest artists. In Harvard Square, **Longfellow House** (105 Brattle Street, Cambridge, 617-876-4491) has chamber music concerts in the garden on alternate summer Sunday afternoons (3 PM).

SECRET COD

What can I say about the **Sacred Cod**? Hanging in a stately fashion over the Massachusetts House of Representatives, the Cod is . . . sacred. Here's how it got that way: on March 17, 1748, John Rowe, a member of the House of Representatives, made a motion before the legislators that "leave might be given to hang up a representation of a Cod Fish in the room where the House sits, as a memorial of the importance of the Cod Fishery to the welfare of the nation."

Yes, in New England, the cod was God: Some say it was the big fish that led to the discovery of America by Basque fishermen while Columbus "was still in knee britches." (Why didn't they tell anyone? Because they wanted to keep those vast fishies all for themselves.) The 17th-century Puritans survived on cod. In the 18th century, Boston grew rich on it — to the point where the British (obviously jealous) coined the phrase "codfish aristocracy" to refer to its troublesome colony.

Originally hung in the Old State House, with the completion of the new *State House* in 1895, the Sacred Cod was moved with all pomp and circumstance to its current home. By the 20th century, so lodged in Boston ways was the Cod that, when the icon was "codnapped" for several days in April 1933 by members of the Harvard Lampoon, the House refused to go about its business until the holy fish was returned.

Now, in a Nietzschean twist of fate (if you'll pardon the pun), Cod is dead. New England's cod fisheries have been all but wiped out by factory trawlers and electronic fishing fleets. Fishing restrictions over the past decade have nearly crushed the region's 300-year-old fishing industry but have helped the cod rebound in local waters to a certain extent. Yet, through it all, the Sacred Cod remains — a reminder of an era when cod ruled the waves, and the pocketbooks, of New England. Pay your homage to the Sacred Cod at the **State House** (Beacon Street, 617-727-3676). Guided tours are offered Monday to Saturday (10 AM to 3:30 PM); free.

SECRET
COFFEE

As a sea captain in the United States Merchant Marine for most of his many years, Jack Logan roasted his own blend of coffee for himself and his crew. Now retired, the white-haired master mariner shares his love of the brew with anyone who happens into his North Square roasterie, **Captain Jack's Best Coffee** (38A Fleet Street). When I passed by one summer day, I met Taylor, one of the crew. She offered advice on choosing a blend: "The yirgacheffe will keep you until 7 PM." I wondered how she knew with such precision. "Captain Jack, we have a new customer," she chirped. But Jack's not one for idle chitchat. "Mm," says he. Anyway, I got my coffee — the kind of cup that makes you sit up and know life is good. A light breeze was blowing through the tiny café and Captain Jack had the radio tuned to something classical. Taylor was more than willing to chat while she cooked up condiments for tomorrow's breakfast. A perfect complement to Jack's best, the crew serves taquitos: Tex-Mex omelettes, made in combinations of 30 or so ingredients, and served in a hot tortilla.

As far as the rest of the North End goes, it's java-topia. The best approach is to wander down **Hanover Street** and check out the wares. If you're a visitor to the North End, count your blessings. You have the luxury of sampling any and all of the many Italian coffee shops here. Locals have to stay loyal to *their* caffe.

The denizens of Davis Square, Somerville, could be said to be on a permanent caffeine buzz. This trend-o-matic square must have the highest concentration of coffeehouses in the region, and each has its distinct disposition. **Diesel Café** (257 Elm Street, Somerville, 617-629-8717) is a haven for those who prefer their coffee muscular, served with a come-as-you-really-are attitude. This GLBT-friendly establishment has pool tables in the back, red vinyl booths, and glass garage doors that open to the sidewalk on mild days. All that, along with fresh food and great hot and cold drinks, makes this the best coffeehouse in Greater Boston. On the opposite side of Davis, the **Someday Café** (51 Davis Square, Somerville, 617-623-3323) is large and loungy, complete with yesteryear's den furniture and Rasta overtones. **Carberry's** (187 Elm Street, Somerville, 617-666-2233) is a local chain whose Davis branch does business on the quieter side of the square. A catchall place, its best features are its big sandwiches and pastries and its collection of sidewalk tables.

In Cambridge, the original **1369 Coffee House** (1369 Cambridge Street, Cambridge, 617-576-1369) in Inman Square, once a great little jazz club, now lives on as a great little coffee shop. There's a clone in Central Square (757 Massachusetts Avenue, 617-576-4600). Also in Central is the pleasantly rumpled **Cezanne** (424 Massachusetts Avenue, 617-547-9616). It's an inspiring space with lofty ceilings and high brick walls where impressive art shows are often hung. The best tables are in the sunny windows overlooking the daily world's fair that constitutes Central Square. In Harvard Square, **Café Paradiso** (see "Secret Ice Cream") has a Euro flavor and especially good chai (spiced tea), as well as all the usual coffee suspects, sandwiches, and homemade gelato.

On Charles Street, the brisk little **Café Vanille** (Charles and Mt. Vernon streets, 617-523-9200), set in a wing of the Charles Street Meeting House, has terrific pastries. The laid-back **Panificio** (144 Charles Street, 617-227-4340) has standard coffee, but the stay-all-day atmosphere makes up for that, and it's a handy compromise spot when one of your party wants booze and the other caffeine. So is Newbury Street's **Other Side Cosmic Café** (407 Newbury Street, 617-536-9477). On the rump end of Newbury Street, this boho coffee shop/café has a terrace that looks out over the Mass Turnpike and a skylit balcony furnished with frumpy armchairs. Open daily (until 1 AM).

Be sure to wander down Warren Street when you visit Charlestown. Among the restored buildings you'll find **Sorelle Bakery & Café** (1 Monument Avenue, at Warren Street, 617-242-2125) with a list of coffee drinks as long at the Bunker Hill Monument is tall, as well as cakes, cookies, and fresh-cut sandwiches. There's a small umbrella terrace, as well as café tables inside, or you can belly up to the bakery bar and chat with the staff.

SECRET
COMEDY

Maybe it's the cruddy weather. Maybe it's the fact that the Sox just can't win. Maybe it's how seriously we take ourselves on a day-to-day basis, being the Athens of America and all that. Whatever the reason, if you come to Boston, prepare to laugh.

There are a number of stand-up venues to choose from, but for local talent, head to the **Comedy Studio** (The Hong Kong, 1236 Massachusetts Avenue, Harvard Square, 617-661-6507). Located above the Hong Kong restaurant (yes, they do serve scorpion bowls) and hosted by the redoubtable Rick Jenkins, this feast of stand-up comics and improv troupes is Boston's freshest. Many of the comics who have played here have since gone on to bigger venues; several have appeared on national television. So you're as likely to see the next big thing returning home to his alma mater as a very funny high school kid whose proud parents sit in the audience. And you are definitely in Cambridge: the halls of academia are a more frequent topic of ridicule than sports. Political humor is also sharp here, and gay, lesbian, and bisexual comics are not only welcome, but required. I love the hilarious **Brian & Mal Show** (www.brianandmal.com), featuring Brian Jewell and Karen "Mal" Malme, who send up life in the queer

lane here and at other venues around town. Comedy Studio shows happen Thursday to Sunday (8 PM). All this and Chinese food, too.

Perhaps because of their seat-of-the-pants approach to theater in general (see "Secret Theater"), improvisational comedy troupes tend to do well in Boston. **ImprovBoston** (Back Alley Theatre, 1253 Cambridge Street, Cambridge, 617-576-1253) has been around for more than a decade. These days, it is both a performance space for various improv troupes and the name of the city's longest running improvisers, who do their thing on Saturdays (8 PM and 10 PM). On other nights, look for Theater Sports, women's improv, and such; $5 to $12. **Improv Asylum** (216 Hanover Street, 617-263-6887) does both improv and sketch comedy at its prime location in the North End. Shows run Wednesdays and Thursdays (8 PM), and Fridays and Saturdays (8 PM and 10 PM), with an additional show on Saturdays (6 PM). Look also for sightings of the very silly, very funny *Musical! The Musical* (www.spontaneousbroadway.com), a peripatetic company that uses audience suggestions to turn a book, story, play, or movie into a musical. The cast — composed of the city's best and brightest improvisers — develops a full-length, Broadway-style musical, complete with accompaniment. Past shows have brought to life the likes of *Silence of the Lambs, The Musical,* complete with a tap-dancing Hannibal Lecter.

SECRET
CRUSTACEANS

Boston's Puritans may have thought lobsters fit only for pigs, but modern diners have other plans for this clawed crustacean. **James**

Hook & Co. (15–17 Northern Avenue, 617-423-5500), right on the waterfront by the old Northern Avenue Bridge, is the oldest lobster monger in the country. It started way back in 1925 and hasn't let up since, every year shipping out some $12 million in *homarus americanus* all over the world. Here at home, you can stop by and peer into Hook's bubbling tanks of seawater, pick out your own multi-pounder, and even get tips from knowledgeable staff on how to cook it. They'll also pack up a lobster for a long trip home. Look as well for shellfish like quahogs (large clams, pronounced "co-hogs"), cherrystones (a half-sized quahog), little necks (a small quahog for eating raw), and mussels, as well as take-out lobster salad rolls.

A little slice of Maine in the heart of Cambridge, **Alive & Kicking Lobsters** (269 Putnam Avenue, Cambridgeport, 617-876-0451) is a new fish store and lobster pound. It's got all the trappings, right down to the wire-box lobster cages stacked in the parking lot and picnic tables under the shade of a vine. This urban lobster shack offers take-home seafood, including fresh-caught haddock, cod, sole, swordfish, tuna, and the company's signature "alive and kicking" lobster, as well as steamers and crabs. They also invite patrons to stick around for a lobster salad sandwich ($9.95) in the picnic area. If all goes as planned, the place will soon add chowder to the menu, as well as steamed lobsters. Bring a bib.

SECRET
CY YOUNG

☙

The coed at the Northeastern University information desk wanted to know what this "Cy Young" statue looked like, because there are like

50 statues on campus, OK? "Um. It's a baseball player," I said. So, heave a sigh for Cy, then do visit him where his effigy stands on the **site of baseball's first World Series** on the former Huntington Avenue Baseball Grounds. The year was 1903 when the famed pitcher led the Red Sox (then called the Pilgrims) to victory against the Pittsburgh Pirates. The last reminder of that moment in sporting history is this bronze Cy Young, winding up in the oval courtyard of Churchill Hall. I dare you to stand in front of him — say, right about where home plate would have been — and look him in the eye.

SECRET
CYCLING

Named after the father of modern cardiology, the **Dr. Paul Dudley White Bike Path** is an easy 18-mile loop hugging the Charles River from the Museum of Science to the Watertown Bridge and back. It's best to start in Watertown, where parking is easier. This area is the prettiest section, too, of this fascinating urban bike ride. Here in Watertown, running through a narrow strip of the Charles River Reservation, the path follows banks cloaked in purple loosestrife and Queen Anne's lace. Be sure to stop along the boardwalks and listen for bullfrogs and bird life. Right along the path, just west of Watertown Square, there's the almost-Art-Deco Metropolitan District Commission swimming pool.

In excellent condition, the **Pierre Lallement Bike Path** (Southwest Corridor Linear Park) is a flat five-mile path coursing through a landscaped linear park, which traces the former route of the elevated

MBTA Orange Line (now rerouted underground). Beginning just outside Copley Place, the path takes riders through the stately South
End to the Arnold Arboretum, Franklin Park, or the Forest Hills T
station, where you can easily make your way back by train (see MBTA,
below).

Traversing the towns of Arlington, Lexington, and Bedford, the
Minuteman Bikeway (Friends of the Minuteman Bikeway, Arlington,
781-641-4891) is a superb 10.5-mile trail built along an old railway
right of way. At first glance, the path looks relatively level, but a trek
from Arlington west will demonstrate the fact that central Boston lies
in a basin 200 feet lower than the surrounding townships. Just throw it
into gear and pedal. From Arlington east, the trail continues another
mile into Somerville as the Linear Park.

As the rails-to-trails program gains momentum in the coming years,
look for two new additions to urban biking. The **East Boston
Greenway** will run from Piers Park to Belle Isle Reservation, and the
Neponset River Greenway will start in Lower Mills and follow the
Neponset River until it empties into Dorchester Bay. Mass Highway
(www.state.ma.us/mhd/paths/bikep.htm) is developing a handy online
library of maps for the trails mentioned above.

The **Middlesex Fells Reservation** (781-662-5230) and the **Blue
Hills Reservation** (visitors' center, 695 Hillside Street, Milton, 617-
698-1802) welcome mountain bikers on designated trails from mid-
April to December. Maps for the Fells are sold at the Map Shack (253
North Avenue, Wakefield, 781-213-7989) and Bookends (559 Main
Street, Winchester, 781-721-5933). At Blue Hills, stop by the visitors'
center. It's open dawn to dusk, but maps are usually available outside
the center at all hours.

In a boon to city bike riders, the MBTA (617-222-3200) has recently
begun offering better access to public transportation for cyclists. The

T no longer requires a permit to bring a bicycle on the Blue, Red and Orange lines and the Commuter Rail outside of peak commuting hours. Bikers can also expect more parking at T stations throughout the city.

Among many other places, you can rent bikes at **Community Bicycle Supply** (496 Tremont Street, 617-542-8623) and ATA **Cycle** (1773 Massachusetts Avenue, 617-354-0907) with prices at around $5 per hour and $20 per day. If you need a fix, there is **Broadway Bicycle School** (351 Broadway, Cambridge, 617-868-3392), where you can get all the help you need to do it yourself (rental tools, assistance, new and used parts) or leave it for them to make it all better. They also sell new and used bikes.

Boston Bike Tours (Tremont Street, between Park Street station and the Boston Common Visitor Information Center, 617-308-5902) offers guided, two- and three-hour bicycle sightseeing tours of Boston and Cambridge, which depart from *Boston Common* Monday to Saturday (1 PM to 3 PM and 4 PM to 6 PM; $18), and Sundays (11 AM to 3 PM; $25) from mid-April through most of October. They also rent city cruisers, hybrids, and mountain bikes ($5 per hour, $25 per day).

S E C R E T
DINERS

A glance at the specials board at the 1940s-era **Deluxe Town Diner** (627 Mt. Auburn, Watertown, 617-924-9789) reveals that it "serves only nice people who enjoy good food." Another row of letters proclaims: "No iceberg here." Those two aphorisms sum up what the

Town Diner is all about: a classic diner setting — ceramic tiles, sparkling soda counter, bottomless coffee, and blue plate specials — with a twist. Owner Don Levy, formerly of the Blue Diner, has thrown a whole new set of fresh and sometimes exotic ingredients into the typical mix. On a recent trip, I sampled a tasty tuna stir-fry with shitake mushrooms and bok choy over udon noodles. The Caesar salad with polenta croutons was generous and lemony and the chef didn't shy away from the anchovy, nor did he overdo it. Yucca fries with chipotle sauce were sweet and crispy. There's a kids' menu as well as a long list of daily specials and blue plates ranging from $7.50 to $8.95. Top off the meal with a traditional dessert like carrot cake, raspberry cheesecake, or chocolate layer cake. Open daily (6 AM to 10 PM).

Kelly's Diner (682 Broadway, Ball Square, 617-623-8102), on the other hand, makes no bones about iceberg lettuce. This Jerry O'Mahoney chrome-sided dining car — built in 1953 in a vaguely Art Deco style — got a new lease on life in 1996 when a Somerville family discovered it in Delaware and carted it up to Ball Square. It still has its Seebury "Wall-o-Matic" jukebox, fed by individual stations at all of the booths. As for the food, this is your basic diner chow served by seasoned waitresses. Breakfast is something of a phenomenon here, with queues of twenty-somethings snaking out onto Broadway on weekend mornings for stacks of hotcakes and bottomless Bundt coffee. Open Monday to Saturday (5:45 AM to 3 PM), and Sundays (6 AM to 2 PM).

No longer a true diner, but worth noting because it's one of Boston's few very-late-night restaurants, the **Blue Diner** (150 Kneeland Street, 617-695-0087) was once the most famous diner in town. Now it's moved one door down to an industrial space that's been decorated to look like a diner. It is still the best place to go for decent food in the wee hours ($4 to $13). Open Sunday to Thursday (11 AM to 4 AM), and all night Fridays and Saturdays. Next door, in the Blue Diner's former aluminum space, is the **South Street Diner** (178 Kneeland Street, 617-350-0028), a casually run, 24-hour eatery.

SECRET
"DOCTOR DEATH"

What, might you ask, has Jack Kevorkian — also known as "Doctor Death" and currently serving a 10- to 25-year prison term in his home state of Michigan — got to do with Boston? The connection is the **Armenian Library and Museum of America** (65 Main Street, at Church Street, Watertown, 617-926-2562), five miles from downtown, where *The Doctor Is In: The Art of Jack Kevorkian* is on permanent display.

Jack Kevorkian is an Armenian-American; his parents were survivors of the Armenian Genocide of 1915–1922. Known as an assisted suicide activist, Kevorkian, it turns out, is a Renaissance man who speaks several languages, paints, writes limericks, plays the flute and harpsichord, and, to his credit, is not at all immune to irony. The doctor's graphic, at times psychedelic, acrylics take their themes from Kevorkian's two preoccupations: music and death. Among the pictures is a portrait of Johann Sebastian Bach, Kevorkian's "personal idol," as well as freaky visual illustrations of musical passages. In the death category, "Very Still Life" depicts a skull with a luminescent white lily rising from its yawning eye socket. In "Nearer My God to Thee," a terrified soul descends into darkness as he grips the sides of a chasm while his fingers fray to bloody stumps. The accompanying literature reveals that Kevorkian sees his paintings not as art but as political commentary aimed at those who persist in seeing "life in the world as a treacly 'Eden,' in this brutal century of horrendous world wars, genocides, and moral anomie."

In addition to his paintings and publications, Kevorkian has contributed a collection of memorabilia to the exhibit. Among the items are a "Kevorkian for President" bumper sticker and a campaign button that reads "Doc Kevorkian for White House Physician." The museum shop sells prints of the doctor's artwork ($175 to 250). Open Tuesdays (1 PM to 5 PM and 7 PM to 9 PM), Fridays and Sundays (1 PM to 5 PM); $2.

SECRET

DOCUMENTARIES

Tinseltown it ain't, but Boston has a thriving documentary film tradition. Errol (*Thin Blue Line*) Morris, Frederick (*Titicut Follies*) Wiseman, and Ross (*Sherman's March*) McElwee are the holy trinity of Boston documentary filmmaking. Given the climate, anyone with a lick of interest should find ample encouragement to sign up for courses at the **Boston Film/Video Foundation** (1126 Boylston Street, 617-536-1540), or **Cityscape** (Filmshack, 227 Roxbury Street, 617-983-5200), where participants earn their credits and learn filmmaking on ongoing film projects. To keep the inspiration flowing, watch for frequent screenings of new and retrospective documentaries at the BF/VF (above), the **Harvard Film Archive**, and the **Museum of**

Fine Arts; or visit the documentary aisle at Brookline's spiffy new **CinemaSmith** (see "Secret Movies").

SECRET

DOG DAYS

"Do dogs really eat these?" asks a mystified customer at a neighborhood bakery. "Oh, yeah," says the cashier. "Did you read the ingredients? How could they not love it?" Even human bakeries are cashing in on the milk bone craze, offering their own in-house doggy biscuits. But no one has as many canine treats as **Fi-Dough** (70E Beacon Street, Somerville, 617-661-3436), whose raison d'être is its doggy deli cases stacked with frosted treats from lobster tail "cookies" to "bagels," "French fries," "ginger snaps," and "peanut butter buns." They also sell all sorts of pet paraphernalia. There's a second location in Beacon Hill (103 Charles Street, 617-723-3266).

Dogs walk their owners anywhere in the city they can find a patch of soothing grass, but to really stretch out, they love Milton's 6,000-acre **Blue Hills Reservation** (visitors' center, 695 Hillside Street, Milton, 617-698-1802) and Medford's 2,000-acre **Middlesex Fells Reservation** (781-662-5230). The most sociable walks are right in the city. Along the Charles River Esplanade, Back Bay, look for the Lotta Crabtree Fountain (Storrow Drive). A retired actress donated this memorial in 1937. There's a drinking fountain for dogs in the base. At **Fresh Pond Park** (Cambridge), leashes can be dispensed with along a two-mile path. There's a grassy area near the entrance where dogs and their friends congregate.

There are dozens of mutt-centric events throughout the year. On the last Sunday in August, Frog Pond is the site of the annual **Boston Common Dog Wash**, a fundraiser hosted by Tufts University School of Veterinary Medicine (508-839-7910); $5. The third Sunday in September, the Massachusetts Society for the Prevention of Cruelty to Animals (MSPCA Walk headquarters, 617-541-5082) has its annual **Walk for the Animals: "Mutts 'n Fluff 'n' Stuff Day,"** a fundraiser for its shelters. Finally, get your dog's **picture taken with St. Nick** at the Boston Animal Rescue League (10 Chandler Street, 617-426-9170, ext. 119) on the first Saturday in December (10 AM to 2 PM).

Do dogs have souls? Hey, you never know. As insurance, get your canine companion **blessed** during National Be Kind to Animals Week (first week in May) at the Boston Animal Rescue League open house, when a priest shows up to administer blessings (617-426-9170, ext. 119). Don't fret if your dog isn't Catholic. All faiths are welcome.

S E C R E T
DRAGONBOATS

Commemorating the life of Chinese poet Qu Yuan, who lived in the third century BC, the **Hong Kong Dragonboat Festival** (Boston Children's Museum, 617-426-6500, ext. 778) is the biggest annual celebration of Asian culture in New England.

The races take place throughout the day (9 AM to 5 PM) between JFK Street and Western Avenue, turning the Charles into a colorful regatta of 40-foot-long teak boats decorated with dragon heads and tails of

gold, red, and green. Vying for top honors, local crews sponsored by high-tech companies, and guest racers from New York and Montreal, compete in teams of 18 paddlers along with a steerperson who beats a large drum in the stern. The boats dock on the Boston side of the river, where teams spend the day carbo-loading, warming up, and getting psyched for the races.

Meanwhile, on the Cambridge side of the Charles along Memorial Drive, a cultural festival spills out (noon to 5 PM) around the Weeks Footbridge. Under the big tent there is continuous entertainment — traditional Chinese and Cambodian dance, taiko drumming, and kung fu demonstrations. Children can make miniature dragons out of recycled foam from the Children's Museum, take a Chinese yo-yo workshop, get their faces painted in ferocious colors, play in a tots' splash pool, or challenge a kid their own age to a game of Chinese checkers. Food stalls representing some of the city's Asian communities line Mem Drive. Be sure to try zung-ze, a rice dumpling wrapped in tea leaves. Chinese legend says that when the beloved poet Qu Yuan threw himself in the river as a political protest, the people tossed these savories into the water to keep the fish away from his body. Today in China, throwing zung-ze into the river remains a tradition.

SECRET
EMERALD NECKLACE

The brainchild of Frederick Law Olmsted, Boston's Emerald Necklace is a strand of nine glittering green spaces stretching from the downtown area through Brookline and Jamaica Plain to Roxbury. Olmsted did not design all of the baubles along the Necklace, but it was his vision to unite established parks with new green spaces as a complete system ringing the city. The nearest of these great parks are standard fare in any visitors' guidebook, but further out on the strand is a world of parklands enjoyed chiefly by those lucky residents who live around them. You're welcome to join the fun.

The oldest public open space in the United States, **Boston Common** was founded in 1634 as a place for Bostonians to graze their "cattel," train their soldiers, bury their dead, and attend public hangings. What can I say? The Puritans had a different idea of leisure from ours today. In the 19th century, public hangings had gone out of style and Victorian reformers had long since banished the last cow. The Olmsted firm (by now run by his sons) made some nips and tucks in the landscape and this once utilitarian space became the Boston Common we know today, an almost-anything-goes leisure space where you can play Frisbee, take a nap, see Shakespeare performed, ice skate, or — as Amelia Bloomer proved in 1851 — climb on a park bench and tell the world what's on your mind.

All of which you cannot do across Charles Street in the **Public Garden**. The nation's oldest public botanical garden, created in 1837, this former salt marsh boasts the world's shortest suspension bridge, which spans a lagoon where pedal-powered **swan boats** (617-522-1966) have been a summer fixture for 125 years. In the northeast corner (near Charles and Beacon streets) the *Make Way for Ducklings* statue pays tribute to Robert McCloskey's Newbury Award-winning children's classic. Well-tended paths meander throughout this 24-acre formal garden past color-coded flowerbeds, corkscrew topiary, flowering trees, fountains, and statuary. With its great trees and heroic monuments, the Public Garden was made for quiet introspection and perhaps a little romance. No public lecturing, no Frisbee, and definitely no napping, please.

Stretching from Arlington Street to the Fens is **Commonwealth Mall**. "Spine" of the elegant Back Bay neighborhood and created by landfill in the 19th century, this narrow, 32-acre band of green was designed to imitate the great boulevards of Haussman's Paris. But you won't find *haute couture* boutiques and tearooms here. Instead, along with a series of statues, monuments, and park benches are scores of mature sweetgum, ash, maple, linden, and elm trees flanked by elegant Victorian townhouses; it's strictly residential. The statue of Norse explorer Leif Ericson (c. AD 970–1020), located at Charlesgate, tends to raise an eyebrow or two. The monument pays tribute to this son of Eric-the-Red; some believe Leif was the first European to explore North America.

From the Mall, one crosses over the Massachusetts Turnpike to reach the first of the Olmsted parks, the **Back Bay Fens**. Looking at the park today, it's difficult to conceive that when Olmsted tackled this space, it was a festering sewage ditch. Olmsted returned the area to its pre-Victorian state as a wild, verdant tidal marsh, adding a series of rough-hewn stone bridges. Today, while the park is still a delight, not much remains of the original Olmsted plan except a couple of bridges. The highlights these days are the tame but lovely **Fenway Victory Gardens**, begun during World War II and now one of the city's most prolific community gardens, and the 1930s **James P. Kelleher Rose Garden** (see "Secret Horticulture") across from the Museum of Fine Arts. The Fens still support a reedy marsh, though now of freshwater rather than salt because of the 1910 damming of the Charles River. The area remains a prime place for spotting birds. (Is it urban legend? The tall reeds are also said to be a trysting area for those with alternative sexual preferences. I don't think that was in the original Olmsted plan any more than the Rose Garden, but times change.)

The next links in the Necklace are a beautiful linear park called the **Riverway**, followed by **Olmsted Park** (Brookline Parks, 617-730-2145). Like the Fens, the Riverway is a completely Olmsted-made environment. Here, the landscape architect created a leafy river glen out of former swampland. Nowadays, the Riverway serves as a tranquil corridor for commuters on foot and joggers. At Olmsted Park, in contrast, the park's namesake made only minor changes to an already attractive landscape, opening up views, laying pathways and sprucing up the existing features of the land.

The only official cycling path in the Emerald Necklace begins at the northern end of Olmsted Park and carries on along popular **Jamaica Pond**, described by Olmsted as "shaded by fine natural forest growth to be brought out overhangingly, darkening the water's edge." The circular pond remains a treat, though a busy one on sunny days, when walkers and joggers flock to the waterside path. The 50-foot-deep pond is fed by springs, making it the purest body of water in Boston. The state stocks the pond with trout, so it's a prime spot for a bit of city fishing. In addition to the trout, you might pull in some of the pond's indigenous pond-food, such as pickerel, bass, and perch. The **boathouse** (617-522-6258) rents sailboats ($20 per hour) and rowboats ($10 per hour). There are concerts at the bandstand as well as seasonal activities. Not to be missed, the ethereal **Lantern Parade** takes place here each Halloween season, when families walk around the pond with homemade lanterns fashioned out of soda bottles covered with bits of colored tissue paper. The event is sponsored by Spontaneous Celebrations (617-524-6373).

Laid out in 1878 by Olmsted and Charles Sprague Sargent, the **Arnold Arboretum** (125 Arborway, 617-524-1717) is the best preserved of

Olmsted's Boston landscapes. One of the city's most beautiful idylls, the 265-acre arboretum is used by Harvard University for the study of flora. It stars some 14,000 trees along with 4,000 plants representing every temperate region in the world. Volunteers lead free tours (617-524-1718) periodically throughout the year. You may find yourself paired with an amateur gardener, a botany student, or a medical writer — but they all have in common an enthusiasm for this garden of great trees. At the Hunnewell building, pick up a catalog of the short courses sponsored by the arboretum, from "tree poetry" to "An Introduction to Lichens." There's also a bookshop here. The grounds are open daily year round from sunrise to sunset.

The largest gem on the Emerald Necklace is **Franklin Park** (Ranger Station, 617-635-7383), weighing in at 500 acres. Olmsted designed this space as a bucolic escape for city dwellers, but over the years it's suffered from both neglect and overzealous development. It's improved over the last few years and offers a wealth of recreational perks, such as African-themed **Zoo New England** (617-442-2002), four and a half miles of paved paths through woods and meadows, as well as miles of unpaved hiking trails. An honored Boston tradition, the annual Kite Festival (City of Boston, 617-635-4505, ext. 6311), takes to the skies at Franklin Park each May.

You can walk the Emerald Necklace with the **Boston Park Rangers** (617-635-4505) when they offer their annual guided tour each summer, as well as with the National Park Rangers from the Frederick Law Olmsted National Historic Site (below), who offer their own parks tour. Or, take the seven-mile trek from the Common to Franklin Park solo with the help of *A Guide to the Parks of Boston's Emerald Necklace* published by Boston Parks and Recreation (1010 Massachusetts Avenue, 617-635-4505). The booklet includes a map, useful phone numbers, and directions on how to cross intersections to get from one park to the next (not always obvious). When you reach Franklin Park, it's possible to backtrack to the Forest Hills T station (near the Arnold Arboretum) for the return trip.

To appreciate the genius of the Emerald Necklace and other green legacies of the father of landscape architecture, visit the **Frederick Law Olmsted National Historic Site** (99 Warren Street, at Dudley Street, Brookline, 617-566-1689). Olmsted made Fairsted his home and office from 1883 until his death. Touring the house, you'll see the old offices and the various apparatuses once used to shoot and develop blueprints, as well as photographs and a scale model of the Emerald Necklace that will give you a bird's-eye view of the whole marvelous scheme. The house is also a research facility for all things Olmsted. The park service has spent over a decade restoring and preserving more than 150,000 plans and drawings generated by the firm. The two-acre property surrounding the house is a living catalog in miniature of the types of parkland Olmsted favored, from picturesque to pastoral. The house and grounds are open Friday to Sunday (noon to 4:30 PM) for guided tours.

SECRET
EXPERIENCED
APPAREL

When it comes to the fashion food chain, some of us are bottom-feeders waiting for twice-worn angora sweaters and last season's power suits to be offloaded by wave-riding fashionistas to a handful of consignment boutiques. At the top of the consignment heap, in terms of price and product, is the **Turnabout Shoppe** (30 Grove Street, Wellesley, 781-237-4450) where *haute couture* lines the walls of a rambling Victorian house. Newberries trade their frippery at **Second Time Around** (167 Newbury Street, 617-247-3504) and **The Closet** (175 Newbury Street, 617-536-1919), both worth checking out for their scores of designer items, though neither is as exclusive as the Wellesley shop. **Clothes Encounters** (1394 Beacon Street, Brookline, 617-277-3031) is another wayside home for slightly used fashions, small but packed with the cast-offs of Brookline society. Finally, the **Closet Exchange** (905 Great Plain Avenue, Needham, 781-444-0367) is relaxingly down market. You'll find items from the Gap and its ilk here, and some true bargains in the rotating stock.

Moving further down the fashion food chain, one arrives with a thump at the **Garment District** (200 Broadway, Cambridge, 617-876-5230), a vast warehouse space near MIT that is as much a cheap date as it is a place to shop. Scores of slack-jeaned Gen-Xers prowl the aisles here, deconstructing post-modernism and discussing their color palettes. In addition to hand-me-downs, there are areas devoted to vintage clothing, one-of-a-kind handmade fashions, and working gear (overalls and uniforms), as well as jewelry and accessories. Sales clerks are usually off socializing but are helpful enough when push comes to shove.

Down in the murky depths of the fashion lifecycle, that hapless angora sweater has been sent through the dryer and made its way to **Dollar a Pound**, just below the Garment District (same phone), where orphaned clothing is lumped in a chaotic pile on the floor to the eternal delight of bargain-hunters. Throwing dignity aside, shoppers arm themselves with grocery store bags and bend on hands and knees to sort through the wreckage hoping to discover an overlooked vintage gem or, less ambitiously, something to wear for house clean-ing. You'll also find housewares, books, and records — all superbly organized. Clothing goes for $1.50 a pound, other items $1 a pound; books and records are priced individually but are always cheap. Open weekdays (9 AM to 7 PM) and weekends (7:45 AM to 7 PM).

SECRET

FENWAY PARK

John Updike called it a "lyric bandbox of a ball park." I find it stretching a point, but grungy old **Fenway Park** (617-236-6666) is an indisputable baseball icon. Home of the Boston Red Sox since 1912, Fenway is the oldest pro baseball stadium in America. But the park's days — at least as the official home of the Sox — may be numbered. A new baseball stadium or major renovation of Fenway is in the offing. Fans of Fenway hope the old park will be saved, but no one knows yet what will become of it.

Such ominous news makes **guided tours** of Fenway that much more essential. Your escort will take you into the park's skanky underbelly as well as to places in the lofty air-conditioned heights that bleacher huggers rarely see. Take in the "600 Club," built by former owner Jean Yawkey and so named because it has 600 seats (duh!), towering high over home plate behind sound- and shatterproof glass. Fans pay $33,000 a season for a bank of cushioned seats here. Down on the field, peek into the bullpens and sit in the dugouts. And while you can't scamper onto the field, you can walk its perimeter and come face to face with the 37-foot-high "Green Monster," Fenway's famous

left-field wall pockmarked with hundreds of high flies. The tour also offers a look at the oldest manually operated scoreboard in major league baseball. Tours start from Service Gate D, located on the corner of Yawkey Way and Van Ness Street, and run Monday to Friday from May to September (10 AM, 11 AM, noon, and 1 PM), except when daytime games are scheduled. There's an additional tour (2 PM) on days when no evening game is scheduled.

Until a new stadium is built, Fenway Park remains the place to see the **Boston Red Sox** (box office, 4 Yawkey Way, 617-482-4SOX for touch-tone ticketing, 617-267-1700 for box office hours). Ticket prices range from $18 for the nosebleed zone to $55 for a seat at field level. There's a helpful seating chart at the team's Web site (www.redsox.com/tickets/seating.html). If this seems pricey to you, try taking advantage of the 20 or so discounted home games each year. They're usually the least popular matches, but still, it's baseball, it's Fenway, it's the Sox. For these games, ticket prices range from $9 for the upper bleachers to $15 for a right-field box seat.

SECRET

FESTAS

Saint season in the North End (see "Secret North End") kicks off with the feast of **St. Anthony** (617-635-3911). It's one of the biggest and most jubilant of a dozen Italian "festas" celebrated here each summer. Organized by private clubs, these animated street fairs celebrate martyrs and sages — St. Rocco, St. Lucy, St. Agrippina, and Madonna della Cava, *et al* — with candlelight processions, sing-a-longs, confetti, and lots of tempting Italian food.

St. Anthony's festa centers on **Pizzeria Regina** (see "Secret Pizza"), snaking its way over to Endicott Street. Throughout the two-day fair, there are several processions in which an effigy of Anthony is paraded through the streets as revelers pin money on the statue. But most of the fun happens around the stage, which is painted to look like a basilica and decked with dozens of light bulbs. Music happens all day and into the night at the twinkling bandstand, with middle-aged guys rendering hits from the '70s. Food is everywhere: fried calamari, sizzling sausage swimming in garlic and onion, raw cherrystones slipped from the shell before your eyes, slices of pizza. And for dessert, the "Cannoli girl" will fill a deep-fried pastry shell for you.

Not to be outdone by their cousins, the Italians of Cambridge and Somerville put on an admirable festa as well when **Cosmos and Damian** are honored in mid-September. Held along Cambridge Street, this day-long festival concludes with a candlelit procession, when the twin saints' effigies are marched down Cambridge Street. Information is available at from the folks at Flowers by Sal (716 Cambridge Street, Cambridge, 617-354-7992).

SECRET

FOLK

⚜

A Mennonite choir sings hymns by the fountain on Boston Common, djembe players drum around downtown park benches, and a bluesman wails at Frog Pond. In the subway, the next Tracy Chapman or Bonnie Raitt is trying out her songs on a momentarily captive audience. And in the North End, an earnest sidewalk accordionist plays tunes from *The Godfather*. Folk music is everywhere in Boston. If you visit this musical city, as Madge used to say, "You're soaking in it."

Despite its being quite a few latitudinal degrees above the Mason-Dixon Line, Greater Boston has a fairly kick-ass bluegrass scene, appreciated by a larger number of devotees than you might expect. The radio show **Hillbilly at Harvard** (WHRB, 95.3 FM) keeps the blue flame burning and the airwaves twanging. The **Boston Bluegrass Union** (617-782-2251) brings national touring artists to the Museum of Our National Heritage (33 Marrett Road, Lexington, 781-861-6559) and organizes free monthly **Picking Parties** at the Stagecoach Inn (also called the Groton Inn, 128 Main Street, intersection of Route 119 and Route 40, Groton, 978-448-5614). The region's brick-and-mortar bluegrass nerve center is **Sandy's Music** (896A Massachusetts Avenue, Cambridge, 617-491-2812). In addition to purveying everything from microphones to mandolins, Sandy hosts old-timey picking sessions on Monday nights (8 PM). On Tuesdays, the unsinkable **Cantab Lounge** (738 Massachusetts Avenue, Cambridge, 617-354-2685) hosts a bluegrass night. A featured band kicks off the evening (9 PM), followed by a picking session. Elsewhere in town, **Johnny D's** (17 Holland Street, Somerville, 617-776-2004) frequently hosts bluegrass bands and solo artists from around the country, as does Club Passim (see below).

World music pops up all over town these days. The Cantab, Club Passim, and Johnny D's host bands from Africa, Latin America, Cuba, and Eastern Europe. The main importer of global music, as well as dance, is **World Music** (617-876-4275), which has brought Papa Wemba, the Mahotella Queens, Youssou N'Dour, Noche Flamenca,

Miriam Makeba, Odetta, Cesaria Évora, Ibrahím Ferrer, and many others to venues all over town, from the 650-seat Paradise Rock Club to the 2,800-seat Orpheum Theater. Tickets range from $20 to $30.

Many of these world and bluegrass venues are hot spots for acoustic music as well. But for the purist, there is nothing like **Club Passim** (47 Palmer Street, Cambridge, 617-492-7679), a 125-seat Harvard Square hole-in-the-ground. In its original incarnation as a jazz club, Passim launched the career of a 17-year-old named Joan Baez. Over the years, scores of folk musicians have got their start here: Tom Rush, Judy Collins, Suzanne Vega, Taj Mahal, Patty Larkin, Nanci Griffith, Shawn Colvin. And while Bob Dylan never headlined, he did play between sets. Concerts at Club Passim are world famous among folkies, but few people know about the music school here. In addition to guitar classes, there is a course in the rich folk music history of Cambridge in which the club played such a vital part. Also on tap are short workshops featuring veteran musicians on such topics as the art of busking or "how to get a gig."

Neighborhood coffeehouses offer a roll of the dice; could be a tone-deaf accountant, could be the next great thing. Look for listings in the *Globe's* Wednesday "Calendar," or check out the **Paradox Lounge** (Puppet Showplace Theatre, 32 Station Street, Brookline, 617-547-7904), **Squawk Coffeehouse** (Harvard-Epstein Church, 1555 Massachusetts Avenue, Cambridge, 617-868-3661), and **Java Jo's** (556 Adams Street, Milton, 617-698-6400). Also look for acoustic and world music festivals, and songwriting workshops, at the **Cambridge Center for Adult Education** (42 Brattle Street, Cambridge, 617-547-6789).

An essential resource for all things folk in Boston is WUMB (91.9 FM, www.wumb.org).

SECRET

FOOTBALL

American football was invented at Harvard University. Well, sort of. The game, in which players could pick up the ball, run with it, and pass it, developed out of soccer at Boston Latin and other area prep schools during the 19th century. When the prep boys became Harvard men, they continued to play by local rules, eventually convincing Yale to do it their way. At the first game, Yale was reported to have shown "very little discipline on the field," i.e., they were clueless. By the next season, the boys from New Haven had got it down and proceeded to beat the leather leggings off Harvard, winning the next 13 games. Today, the rivalry continues and the **Harvard-Yale game** (Harvard Athletics ticket office, 617-495-2211) is one of the highlights of the college sports year.

SECRET

FRENCH

Francophiles get a *frisson* at a handful of Boston landmarks. First stop: the **Paul Revere House** (19 North Square, 617-523-2338). The patriot-silversmith was the son of French immigrants who anglicized the family name, Rivoire, in the 1720s. Over on Boston Common stands the bronze and granite **Lafayette Monument** (along Tremont Street, next to the visitors' center). It was erected in 1924 to commemorate the 150th anniversary of the Marquis de Lafayette's visit to

Boston, when he announced that the King of France would help the colony in its bid for independence. At the **Shirley-Eustis House** (33 Shirley Street, Roxbury, 617-442-2275) a room is dedicated to the marquis, who stayed the night at this grand former governor's mansion.

There is no shortage of very good upscale French restaurants in Boston. But I like to take a vicarious trip to France more than once a year. A couple of crêperies make it affordable. **Le Gamin** (550 Tremont Street, 617-654-8969) offers relatively cheap and good fare. Crêpes, both savory and sweet, are accompanied by a salad of mesclun and vinaigrette. In addition to the classic ham and cheese, there are yummy deviants like turkey and goat cheese. Le Gamin serves other French bistro items for a bit more, including steak au poivre ($17.50). More of a take-out place, **One Arrow Street** (1 Arrow Street, Cambridge, 617-661-2737) has a few tables and a cozy solarium for dining on "thin pancakes." Look for standard French fillings like Nutella (a hazelnut spread), sugar and butter, ham and cheese, and merguez (lamb, veal, and spices). Also on the menu are several innovative combinations. The lemonade, whipped with ice and raspberries or mint, is superb. Open weekdays (10 AM to midnight) and weekends (9 AM to midnight).

The first thing everyone notices about **Sandrine's** (8 Holyoke Street, Cambridge, 617-497-5300) is the knockout façade. This Alsatian bistro has a replica of a Parisian art nouveau Metro sign at its entrance. Inside the décor is less exciting, but disappointments of that sort are quickly forgotten when the food arrives. My ideal Sandrine's meal is a nice Alsatian wine with a flammeküche. Composed of strips of caramelized onions, smoked bacon, and white sauce or other combinations, these pizza-like staples of eastern France are delicious and extremely rich. Even so, don't take a pass on the desserts; they're edible art.

Founded after World War II, the **French Library and Cultural Center** (53 Marlborough Street, 617-266-4351) is the axis of French life in Boston. The library offers conversation, films, events, resources, videos, and French classes to members. The highpoint of the French Library's year is the **Bastille Day Festival,** which takes place on the weekend nearest July 14, complete with a *bal musette* at Café Fleuri and Sunday brunch at Le Meridien Hotel. Reservations are required. Across the river, Harvard Square celebrates liberté, egalité, and gastronomy with a family-oriented **Bastille Day** (Holyoke Street, 617-497-5300) street fair. Sandrine's and other area French restaurants supply the food. The event kicks off with a traditional Parisian-style waiters' race (4 PM).

S E C R E T

FRUITS AND VEGGIES

Not that anyone is going to get her USDA five servings a day this way, but just so you know: a number of Boston neighborhoods have public fruit trees and shrubs thanks to the **Urban Orchards** project. Earthworks (11 Green Street, 617-623-2784) started Urban Orchards a decade ago and has since seen to the planting of more than 500 fruit- and nut-bearing plants in Allston, Dorchester, Jamaica Plain, Roxbury, the South End, Cambridge, and Somerville. Some of these trees and shrubs are found on school lots; others are integrated into community gardens, housing developments, youth centers, public parks, church properties, and abandoned lots. Seek and you may find grapes, raspberries, cherries, gooseberries, nectarines, blueberries, hazelnuts, apples, pears, figs, filberts, blackberries, and plums. Visit Earthworks's Web site (www.gis.net/~erthwrks) for a list of what's out there.

Despite rumors of its demise, **Haymarket** (Blackstone, North, and Hanover streets) is still bustling on the brink of the North End. This celebrated outdoor market has been a Boston fixture since the mid-1970s (though there was a *hay* market in Boston as early as the 1700s). The guys behind the stacks of fruit and veg dress for the job in muscle shirts (if they wear shirts) and keep up a perpetual banter, reeling in customers with calls of "dollar a pound" and "five for a dollar." There's no telling what will turn up at the market from week to week, though you can count on finding staple items like tomatoes, potatoes, onions, limes, bananas, apples, and grapes. Often more exotic items show up, especially since the market is becoming popular with shoppers looking for ethnic produce. Haymarket is open on Fridays and Saturdays all year round (dawn to dusk). Arrive toward 5 PM on Saturday and they'll be practically giving things away. For the best quality and a somewhat calmer pace (100,000 people pass through the market each weekend), show up Friday morning.

While Haymarket produce comes from California and Florida (via the Chelsea Produce Market), **farmers' markets** bring New England bounty to the table. Local produce and flowers start rolling into the city farmers' markets in late spring. The downtown locations are at City Hall Plaza, Government Center, Mondays and Wednesdays (11 AM to 6 PM) and at Copley Square, which goes green on Tuesdays and Fridays (11 AM to 6 PM), when a row of striped awnings pops up along St. James Avenue. Early in the season, look for potted herbs and flowers, baked goods, jams and jellies, and locally made goat cheese. As the summer unfolds, veggies, legumes, and cut flowers come in by the bins and buckets. Both of these markets start in late

May and operate through most of November. For a list of other city farmers' markets, visit the Web site of the **Federation of Massachusetts Farmers' Markets** (www.massfarmersmarkets.org).

Metropolitan Boston's last working farm, **Allandale** (259 Allandale Street, 617-524-1531), sits on a plot of land that's been under cultivation for more than 350 years. The current owners opened their farm stand nearly three decades ago. In addition to what they grow on site, Allandale sells produce from other area growers and offers locally made breads and condiments. Open daily from mid-April through December 23. Further afield, **Verrill Farm** (11 Wheeler Road, Concord, 617-287-0361) provides fresh produce to some of Boston's top restaurants. The shop also offers baked goods, prepared salads, and pick-your-own options as the seasons turn. **Wilson Farms** (10 Pleasant Street, Lexington, 781-862-3900) has shipped-in exotics, as well as heaps of fresh local produce. Look also for condiments and cheeses, as well as goose, duck, turkey, and capon.

In addition to the open-air and farmers' markets, there are a couple of Boston-area grocery stores worth crowing about. In the heart of Little Armenia (see "Secret Armenian"), **Kay's** (594 Mt. Auburn, Watertown, 617-923-0523), the "great green grocer," boasts better prices and fresher produce than you'll find in any chain store. The constant chat of the cigar-chomping owner and his cashiers sets the mood as shoppers squeeze their vegetables or gaze with lust over the selection of Middle Eastern cheeses. Kay (if that's his name) is the kind of guy who can get away with calling his female customers "sweetheart." The male customers get rougher treatment. When a cashier asks a customer, "How's your wife?" Kay chimes in from across the store, "Not good; she's married to him."

Maybe it's something in the water. Not only does Watertown have Kay's, but it also boasts the amazing **A**. **Russo & Sons** (560 Pleasant

Street, Watertown, 617-923-1500). Everything at this West Watertown market is lusher, riper, bigger, juicer. Seasonal produce is the
star: native sweet corn, vine-ripened tomatoes, and vegetables favored
by Asian and Italian cooks — items usually found only in Chinatown
or the North End. While it's not a huge place, the variety is pretty
well stunning. Take, for example, the melon department, where one
day I found no fewer than 10 different types: sharlynne, casaba,
crenshaw, canary, Santa Claus, orange-flesh, cantaloupe, honeydew,
watermelon, and (my favorite) galia. There's a refrigerator case with
Middle Eastern cheeses, Massachusetts milk in one-quart glass bottles,
free-range chicken, and organic sausage. But wait, I haven't told you
about the plants. The bigger, better, lusher tag fits here too. Even after
a nasty heat wave, Russo's hanging petunias glow.

For those on the prowl for the ultimate salad, here are a couple of
green flings. The smell of garlic drifting out onto jp's buzzing Centre
Street announces **Bella Luna Café** (405 Centre Street, Jamaica Plain,
617-524-6060). Once you've read the menu, a choice of pizzas and
Italian-American fare, consider the greens. These (and the homemade
tiramisu) are where this popular (and noisy) eatery excels. Try, for
example, the Silver Moon: mesclun sprinkled with dried cranberries
and bits of gruyere, topped with a subtle dressing. Another brilliant
salad mind can be found at **Gargoyle's on the Square** (219 Elm
Street, Somerville, 617-776-5300), the French bistro that has been
setting a higher tone on Davis Square's Elm Street than anyone previ-
ously imagined could be set. Choose from the seasonal menu or the
specials. You'll find exotic leaves studded with dried fruits and
cheeses and drizzled with savory dressings.

SECRET

GARGOYLES

A perfect July night. The dinner crowd on Newbury Street is whooping it up. Life doesn't get any better than this. Until you die. Reminding Newberries of their essential mortality is a little shop of horrors called **Gargoyles, Grotesques & Chimeras** (262 Newbury Street, 617-536-2362), where the doors creak open just as the lights begin to twinkle down hedonism boulevard. Walk into the crypt-like space for a tour of all that lurks; it's the place your mind goes when you wake up at 4 AM in a cold sweat; it's a prop shop for Stanley Kubrick. It's actually really cool, packed with hellcats and harridans, weathered plaster saints and crucifixes, green men, mummies, egg cartons filled with tiny skulls, and gargoyles gazing down from crusty perches with malevolent, gurgling grins. Also found here: "soul paintings," bluish, ghostly images from the other side. The shops chimerical hours start at around 3 PM (or by appointment).

SECRET

GENIUSES

Being the intellectual hub of the known universe, Boston has had an awful lot of geniuses running around loose throughout its 400-year history. Now these erstwhile eggheads are celebrated in a tour put together by the Boston History Collaborative (617-350-0358) called the **Innovation Odyssey**. This two-hour comfy-bus ride through

Boston's history of invention is led by a professional actor who transforms himself (or herself) into a bewildering array of characters. While the bus takes you from place to place, the guide brings to life some of the city's superlatives and firsts. There is Alexander Graham Bell's invention of the telephone, the first mutual funds (then called Boston Funds), the first e-mail message, the accidental discovery of the microwave oven by radar researchers at Raytheon (the Radarange), and, finally, the decoding of the human genome in Cambridge's "Genetown." Along with better-known events, the tour revives some of the forgotten heroes and heroines of Boston innovation. You'll hear about Ellen Swallow Richards, who taught chemistry at MIT in the 1880s and championed improved sanitary conditions in the city; and Onesimus, an African slave in the service of Cotton Mather, whose tribal practice inspired the New World's first smallpox inoculations in 1721. The visit includes stops at Mass General Hospital's Ether Dome (see "Secret Surgical Theater"), Harvard Yard, and the Pioneer Telephone Museum. Call or check the Web site (www.innovationtrail.com) for times and prices.

In addition to the Pioneer Telephone Museum (which can only be visited through the Innovation Odyssey), Alex Bell is commemorated in several other downtown spots. There's a granite marker in the northwest corner of City Hall Plaza claiming to be "the birthplace of the telephone." Well, sort of. It was in a building on this approximate site that the first *unintelligible* phrase was heard over one of Bell's apparatuses. It wasn't until March 10, 1876, at Exeter Place, that the famous words: "Mr. Watson, come here, I want you!" were heard and the telephone began to wind toward its current ubiquitous place in our lives. A faithful reconstruction of another Bell hangout, his **109 Court Street garret**, is open for public viewing just off the lobby of the Verizon building (185 Franklin Street, Boston). The display includes a replica collection of the telephone's earliest mechanisms: the transmitter-receiver used at Bell's Exeter Place lab that carried the first intelligible speech, the first telephone switchboard. Also, note Dean Cornwell's heroic-style 1950s mural in the lobby, depicting the glorious deeds of *Telephone Men and Women at Work*.

SECRET

GLBT

Boston offers a better climate than many American cities for being yourself. Many gay, lesbian, bisexual, and transgender folks are out at their jobs. Some hold hands or kiss in public — but that depends on the neighborhood. In places like JP, the South End (not to be confused with South Boston), and parts of Cambridge where there are larger numbers of GLBT folks, public affection is fairly routine. But, of course, no place is safe from discrimination, harassment, and the threat of violence. Though Boston homophobes may be less "out" about their feelings, there's no question they are there.

In any case, there is enough of a GLBT community in Greater Boston to make life interesting. The best guides to the cultural scene are found on the Web. The online magazine **Butch Dyke Boy Productions** (www.butchdykeboy.com) lists events in Boston's queer community along with feature articles, commentary, and a must-see links page. If you'd like to get free e-mail updates of Boston events in your inbox each week, sign up at **Queer Agenda** (www.queeragenda.org).

In print, the comprehensive Pink Pages (www.linkpink.com) is an annual A–Z listing of gay-friendly businesses and services, from accessories and window treatments to restaurants and lodging. The free weekly *Bay Windows* is the region's largest newspaper devoted to gay and lesbian national issues and local events. *Bay Windows's* community guide is essential reading for anyone looking for support groups, sports clubs, professional services, and so forth. The monthly *Sojourner* covers the world of women of all persuasions. Both *Bay Windows* and *Sojourner* have extensive arts sections.

All of these resources will point the way to happenings around town. There are, however, some regularly scheduled events I can't fail to point out. **Dyke Night at the Midway Café** (3496 Washington Street, Jamaica Plain, 617-524-9038) is universally hailed as the best lesbian bar in the city. This weekly Thursday event is hosted by activist Kristen Porter (dykenight@hotmail.com), who also concocts events (usually at the Midway) like the ever-popular Drag King Contest, Ms. Boston Leather, and the New Year's Fantasia Ball. In the Theater District, **Friday Night at Circuit Girl** (67 Stuart Street, circuitgirl100@aol.com) is an anything-goes lesbian dance club. The only thing of its kind in Boston, **Gender Crash** (Butch Dyke Boy, butchdykeboy.com) is a semi-monthly spoken word event, a welcoming place for people to try out material. It's held at Spontaneous Celebrations (45 Danforth Street, Jamaica Plain, 617-524-6373).

Anyone looking for gay nightclubs has only to peruse the pages of *In News Weekly* aimed at the young, gay man on the prowl. But for something a bit subtler, check out **Gays for Patsy, Inc.** (781-446-3115). For more than a decade, this social club has been sponsoring gay-friendly line dancing events in Boston. Open to all, its Lambda Ranch (First Church of Jamaica Plain, Centre and Eliot streets) is a smoke-free dance that begins with lessons, be they in Texas two-step, waltz, swing, cha-cha, polka, or plain vanilla line dancing. At the same location, **Jamaica Plain Gay & Lesbian Contra Dancers**

(617-971-0828, JP.Dance@ContraCorner.com) sponsor biweekly contra dances for gays, lesbians, and friends, usually with live music.

Boston's **Pride Week** (June) is a major annual event, with its climactic Gay Pride Parade. But in recent years, the in-your-face attitude that used to make the parade such a high has dimmed. Bostonians mourn the old days when marching in the parade was a political act, now that corporate banners outnumber maverick floats. But grassroots still stir during Pride Week. In the last few years, the **Dyke March** has been doubling in size each year. It takes place the night before the Gay Pride Parade.

Some of the city's edgiest and most innovative theater is produced within the GLBT community. Sponsored by the Theater Offensive, **Out on the Edge** (617-426-2787) is an annual three-week festival of lesbian, gay, bisexual, and transgender theater where viewers can expect just about anything, from drag opera divas to gay fairy tales and lesbian stand-up. The festival offers a forum for regional theater companies. It also attracts nationally known artists who, in addition to performing, offer free workshops during the festival.

S E C R E T
GONDOLAS

"You might say these boats are on the endangered list. They're very rare," says Joseph Gibbons. The newly minted gondolier is owner, along with his wife Camille, of **Gondola di Venezia** (Canal Park, CambridgeSide Galleria, Cambridge, 617-876-2800), which offers gondola rides along the Cambridge Canal out to the Charles River

Basin. The Gibbonses, self-professed "gondolaholics," got interested in the art and history of these boats on a honeymoon trip to Venice, eventually deciding to bring a little bit of Venetian romance home with them. Built on the island of Dorso d'Oro, the Gibbonses' two boats are fashioned out of nine types of wood, from black walnut to mahogany, and feature hand-carved bows and sterns gilded with 24-carat gold. In addition to procuring his *objet d'art* boats, Gibbons spent three weeks in the canals of Venice learning the art of *voga* rowing, a traditional style of gondola piloting.

The price of the 45-minute voyage is $65 for two. To make your joy complete, hire the Milanese accordion player to come along ($70). And bring a bottle of Limoncello. Your gondolier will ice it, open it, and provide glasses. Otherwise, the onboard CD player provides music, or if your pilot's in the mood he might sing a little Puccini. If you go, don't forget: your gondolier works for tips.

S E C R E T
GREEN SPACES

You can hardly miss the venerable Emerald Necklace, Boston's gorgeous strand of parkland running from Boston Common to Franklin Park (see "Secret Emerald Necklace"). But not everyone is aware of the city's many new green spaces scattering, these days, like loose jewels across the landscape.

In the North End, just below the North Washington Street Bridge, the five-acre **Paul Revere Park** (off Causeway Street) has stunning views of the Leonard P. Zakim Bunker Hill Memorial Bridge — or

will when the rusting iron and concrete monster it's replacing is torn down. There's a small amphitheater here, along with stone walls decorated with lettered tiles commemorating the patriot's revered ride. The silversmith crossed the river here to "git me a horse" from Deacon Larkin in Charlestown on that fateful night in 1775. The Metropolitan District Commission Rangers (617-727-1188) do a walking tour called "The Lost Half Mile" on the rebirth of the Charles River Basin, for decades the missing link in Boston's riverside green spaces. This park is the first link in a riverside chain that will grow as the Big Dig (see "Secret Big Dig") comes to completion.

Now nearly a decade old, but young by Boston park standards, **Post Office Square** (Friends of Post Office Square, 617-423-1500) lies in the heart of the Financial District. Occupying a 1.7-acre block surrounded by the Art Deco façades of the Post Office, Le Meridien Hotel, and the old New England Telephone Building, this gem of a park replaced a decrepit concrete parking structure (a new parking garage is now hidden below). Cast-iron benches, trellised walkways, and — astounding for such a postage-stamp-sized park — some 125 varieties of trees and shrubs make this a favorite urban oasis of the office crowd. The Friends of Post Office Square (above) sponsor free lunchtime concerts on the square from May to September (12:15 PM); call for details.

Piers Park (95 Marginal Street, East Boston) is a grand green space offering abundant reasons for outsiders to make the short trek to East Boston on the Blue Line. There are rolling grassy hills for practicing cartwheels, a spurting fountain to cool tired feet, and an elaborate playground as well. Be sure to meander out the long pier to Noddle Island, a stone shelter decorated with fabulous granite carvings, inspired by the art of East Boston's many cultural groups past and present. The name "Noddle Island" commemorates Eastie's pre-landfill life as an archipelago. Across Marginal Street, peek into the well-kept community garden.

Providing a wayside rest for Freedom Trail tourists on their way to *Old Ironsides* is Charlestown's **City Square State Park** (Rutherford and Chelsea streets, 617-242-1065). Surrounded by the roar of traffic, it's not exactly tranquil, but the layout of this acre of earth is so charming you can forgive the brouhaha. A whimsical fountain incorporates figures of fish and birds, while a wayward frog sits nearby. Interpretive signs throughout the park describe the history of this city square, dating back to 1629, and 75 species of deciduous and evergreen trees provide four seasons of color.

Just off Central Square, Cambridge, the 1.3-acre **University Park Common** (Sidney Street) is another new green space. This former industrial area is the property of MIT, which is building dormitories and biotech office space here. The park looks like private property, but its chrome café tables, granite benches, and paths are open to the public. Throughout the park, look for monuments, memorials, and bronze artifacts to factories that once stood here. Pick up a snack at one of Central Square's dozens of ethnic eateries and bring it on down.

It's not new, but I can't miss mentioning Coolidge Corner's diminutive, tucked-away nature preserve, **Hall's Pond Nature Sanctuary** (behind 1120 Beacon Street, Brookline). This five-acre park surrounds a lily-strewn pond with a winding path, just off Beacon Street and totally hidden.

SECRET
HARVARD

Let's put things in perspective. The annual budget of **Harvard University** ($1.8 billion) is larger than that of Honduras ($1.15 billion). It's the oldest institution of higher learning in the United States, founded in 1636, just 16 years after the Pilgrims first bumped into Plymouth Rock. The university boasts 38 Nobel laureates and occupies nearly 5,000 acres of prime real estate in Cambridge, Brookline, and Boston. This is not a university; it's a universe. Take a look at what makes this famous and infamous institution tick on daily **campus tours** with student guides, departing from the Harvard Information Center (Holyoke Center, Cambridge, 617-495-1573). The tours are offered year round, Monday to Friday (10 AM and 2 PM), and Saturdays (2 PM only); free.

After the tour, for those whose ambitions reach no further than the swift purchase of a pair of "Harvard" boxer shorts, the **Harvard Coop** (1400 Massachusetts Avenue, 617-499-2000) is the place to go, as well as the place to "go," as it has one of the few public restrooms in the area. By the way, it's pronounced "coop," as in chicken.

However, it's my duty to tell you that Harvard also has six excellent museums, and they're all open to the public. In addition to the three **Harvard University Art Museums** (see "Secret Art"), the **Peabody Museum of Archaeology and Ethnology** (11 Divinity Avenue, Cambridge, 617-496-1027) has a superb collection of artifacts from North American Indian cultures. There are, as well, three floors of additional archaeological and ethnological exhibits taking in Africa, the Pacific, and Mesoamerica, as well as items from Lewis and Clark's expedition. The Peabody also has a fine gift shop. Open daily (9 AM to 5 PM); $6.50. Free admission, Sundays (9 AM to noon) and Wednesdays during the school year (3 PM to 5 PM).

Showcasing temporary exhibitions on archeological topics, the **Semitic Museum** (6 Divinity Avenue, Cambridge, 617-495-4631), established in 1889, focuses on Arab and Jewish cultures of the Near East. Open weekdays (9 AM to 5 PM); free, though a small fee is sometimes charged for special exhibitions.

At the **Harvard Museum of Natural History** (26 Oxford Street, Cambridge, 617-495-3045), visitors have a chance to explore the collections of the university's departments of botany, zoology, and mineralogy (that is, animals, plants, and rocks). The museum can display only a small portion of its estimated 21 million specimens — most of which, I'm told, are bugs and some of which, I'm also told, make up Vladimir Nabokov's butterfly collection. (Before turning to writing novels full time, Nabokov made a name for himself as a lepidopterist.) Also in the animal kingdom, the museum boasts Kronosaurus — a 42-foot-long, 120 million-year-old skeleton — the largest marine reptile that ever lived.

In the plant realm, there are the famous glass flowers. It's difficult to describe the effect this exhibit creates. While Harvard calls it a "garden," I think that leads potential visitors down the wrong path. Made in Dresden, Germany, between 1836 and 1937, the flowers are stowed under glass and away from glaring lights, making a more studious than artistic impression. But they are quietly awesome, especially for those who take time to view the adjoining exhibit, which shows how a father and son team created them between 1886 and 1937.

It might be more apt to call the museum's mineralogical galleries a garden. In a series of brilliantly lit, expansive rooms, groves of fluorescent yellow sulfur crystals, shimmering purple amethyst, and chunks of precious metals in infinite colors and shapes set a stunning scene.

Throughout this diverse museum, aside from a few interactive stations that pop up at temporary shows, the exhibits are old-style, look-don't-touch displays. But there's nothing cranky or dusty here. And would you believe it? Kids adore this museum. Open daily (9 AM to 5 PM); $6.50. Free admission, Sundays (9 AM to noon) and Wednesdays during the school year (3 PM to 5 PM).

SECRET

HO CHI MINH

Commissioned by Boston Gas in 1971 to adorn its Dorchester Bay gas tanks along the Southeast Expressway, the murals of artist Corita Kent hold a secret. Or maybe not.

When Kent painted the tanks, with splashes of primary colors resembling the strokes of a giant paintbrush, the murals became an instant landmark. Then someone pointed out that on the left side of the blue stripe there appeared to be a profile of Ho Chi Minh, the then-recently deceased founder of Vietnam's Communist Party and president of North Vietnam. Speculations piled up. Kent was a Vietnam War protester. Was this a subliminal message she'd slipped in to provoke the corporate hierarchy?

In the mid-'90s, one of the tanks was razed and the mural on the remaining tank was repainted in such a way that the Ho profile is said to be somewhat less obvious. Boston Gas claimed it was merely following the artist's original plans and continued to deny any resemblance to the communist leader in that much-discussed blue stripe.

Kent died over a decade ago, so we'll never know what her real intentions were, even if she had cared to comment on the controversy. Now owned by Keyspan, the remaining tank can be seen, with or without its mystery Ho (you be the judge), from Route 93, about 10 minutes south of downtown.

SECRET

HORTICULTURE

At its best in mid-June, the **James P. Kelleher Rose Garden** (Back Bay Fens) is an explosion of creamy color, with dozens of varieties of fragrant, flamboyant roses. Most of the flowers are labeled with their star-struck names, and stone benches covered by canvas canopies give admirers a little noonday shade. But don't think you have to wait for a sunny day. Aficionados claim that when the sky is overcast, colors appear brighter and the scents sweeter. Perhaps because its joys are so fleeting, locals are only vaguely aware of this hoard of petals. Mark your calendar now so you won't forget to visit when June rolls around next year. To find the rose garden, enter the Back Bay Fens across from 69 Park Drive or at the corner of Forsyth Way and The Fenway, just behind the Museum of Fine Arts.

In the same park, the **Fenway Victory Gardens** harbor some of the city's longest-established community gardens, having sprouted up during World War II. No longer aiding the war effort (God help us),

Fenway residents are free to grow a frivolous crop of flowers and herbs, often setting up informal patios with chairs and umbrellas.

In addition to the Fenway Victory Gardens, some 250 community gardens can be found all over Greater Boston. Neighborhood residents may wait years to get their own plot, which they feel understandably protective of. So, while sightseers shouldn't enter community gardens, they can always peek over the fence to see black-eyed peas, corn, and okra in Dorchester's Leyland Street Community Garden, or an explosion of perennial flowers and found sculpture in Somerville's Bikeway Community Garden. Once a year, the gardens open their doors to visitors when **Garden Futures** (617-542-7696, www.gardenfutures. org) sponsors a garden bus tour. It's also possible to contact Betsy Johnson at Garden Futures any time for a map showing the locations of all the community gardens. She'll help you set up your own self-guided tour. Anyone interested in urban gardening should check Garden Futures' Web site. In addition to a complete list of community gardens, you'll find valuable resources (where to find free manure!), as well as gardening tips and plant sale announcements.

Another annual garden event, **Hidden Gardens of Beacon Hill** (Beacon Hill Garden Club, 617-227-4392), has been offering a rare glimpse at the diminutive backyards of the Hill since 1929. The self-guided tour takes place the third Thursday in May, and tickets include refreshments; $25. With Beacon Hill's hidden horticultural success, a number of other Boston neighborhoods have begun to mount similar annual events. Among them are **Secret Gardens of Cambridge** (Cambridge Public Library, 617-349-4040) in May, and **Hidden Gardens of Allston-Brighton** (Wilma Wetterstrom, 617-787-9844) in mid-July.

There are weekly garden gatherings from May to October at the funky **Somerville Community Growing Center** (22 Vinal Avenue,

Somerville). Join the e-mail list (write to llicardo@postharvard.edu) and receive cheery notices of what's blooming as well as announcements of happenings from labyrinth walks to outdoor films, open mic nights, nature talks, and performance art. All events are free.

Throughout the growing season, look for plant sales sponsored by the **Arnold Arboretum** (125 Arborway, 617-524-1717). Further out, the **Lyman Estate** (185 Lyman Street, Waltham, 781-891-4882, ext. 244) has an excellent herb sale behind its extensive greenhouses. All the kitchen condiments are represented — basil, oregano, and fennel — as well as edible flowers like nasturtiums and johnny-jump-ups. The greenhouses here are some of the oldest conservatories in the United States. Visit from November to March for the spectacular show of 100-year-old camellia trees. The grounds are open to the public (the house is rented for private functions). The greenhouses are open year round for sales and tours. Closed Sundays.

It doesn't have nearly the variety of the big garden stores, but **Avenue Gardener** (167 Brighton Avenue, 617-782-8555) takes advantage of its small stature by providing personal service. Buying a plant here is more like an adoption process than a commercial transaction. Owner Janet Hawkins cares about green things, and she must have a chartreuse thumb to get things to grow so lushly in this cramped space (that doubles as a used furniture shop), from gloating Venus flytraps to cheery flats of cherry tomatoes for the summer garden. Come also for potting soil, gardening tools, regional gardening magazines, seeds, and copious advice. Closed Mondays.

SECRET
ICE CREAM

Blame your spare tire on Steve Herrell. His parlor in Somerville's Davis Square, Steve's — set up in 1973 in a former dry cleaning store — was the first to serve "premium" ice cream to the masses. Herrell introduced a process that made a richer, smoother ice cream than the typical commercial blend Bostonians were used to consuming. He also introduced mix-ins. The server would plop a scoop of ice cream on a marble tablet, sprinkle it with candies, nuts, or crumbled cookies, stir, then spoon it into a cone or bowl. People loved Steve's. Lines formed, waistlines expanded.

Herrell sold Steve's after four years, but returned to the ice cream business in 1982, setting up **Herrell's** (15 Dunster Street, 617-497-2179) in Harvard Square. It's the same superb Steve's recipe, only "mix-ins" are now called "smoosh-ins." The shop's 70 flavors include classics like maple cream, cappuccino, and cookie dough, as well as out-there flavors like key-lime-cardamom, cashew butter, Kentucky bourbon, and peach schnapps. There is another branch in Allston (155 Brighton Avenue, Allston, 617-782-9599). Both stores are open until midnight.

While Herrell was the first, others have followed, bringing their own twist to the burgeoning trade. Opened in 1981, **Toscanini's** (899 Main Street, Cambridge, 617-491-5877) has rich, creamy ice cream — many people will tell you it's the best in Boston — along with a menu of wild flavors. On any given day, the list might include Earl Grey, green tea, or khulfee (like the Indian dessert with cardamom, ground almonds, and ground pistachios). Among the "standard" flavors are a beautiful gingersnap molasses, excellent coffee ice cream, and a superb caramel chocolate chip. In addition to the Central Square location, there's an outpost at the MIT Stratton Student Center (Building W20, west of Massachusetts Avenue, 617-491-1558) and one just across from Harvard Yard (1310 Massachusetts Avenue, 617-354-2865). Open until 11 PM.

You can't miss JP **Licks** (659 Centre Street, Jamaica Plain, 617-524-6740). Just look for the giant cow's head. Outdoor tables make this the best place to sit and watch Jamaica Plains's Centre Street scene pass by. This is another shop selling very good, always fresh ice cream, with a few exotics in the lineup like cucumber ice cream or Sam Adams cream stout ice cream. The sorbets are also excellent. There are branches in the Back Bay (352 Newbury Street, 617-236-1666), at Coolidge Corner (311 Harvard Street, Brookline, 617-738-8252), and at Newton Center (46 Langley Road, 617-244-0666). Open until midnight.

A couple of other ice cream shops of note are **Ice Creamsmith** (2295 Dorchester Avenue, 617-296-8567), at the base of Dot Ave in Lower Mills, which makes a dozen or so classic flavors and a couple of frozen yogurts. The ice cream is good, and the prices are lower than those of most other homemade ice cream shops. Open daily from March to November (noon to 10 PM). **Christina's** (1255 Cambridge Street, 617-492-7021) has 75 flavors, with perhaps 50 of them available on any given day. The ice cream is tops, and their exotics are really out there, including challenging flavors like clam chowder.

The home of the homemade gelato is **Café Paradiso** (253 Hanover Street, 617-742-1768). Less fattening than premium ice cream, but bursting with flavor, gelato is also softer because it is stored and served at slightly higher temperatures than ice cream. The flavors run from amaretto to hazelnut to espresso, pistachio, and lemon (which is dairy free). Paradiso's gelato is also served where it's made at the Harvard Square Café Paradiso (1 Eliot Square, Cambridge, 617-868-3240). The North End café is open until 2 AM and the Harvard Square outpost until midnight.

And now a word about **milkshakes**: in Boston, they do not contain ice cream. If I'd known this when I moved here as a grad student craving a tall cold chocolate one from time to time, I would have avoided much disappointment. So I'm telling you now. To get what the rest of the world considers a milkshake, ask for a "frappe" (pronounced "frap"). Otherwise, you'll get a nice glass of chocolate milk. Yuck! Any of the places above will shake up an excellent one for you.

SECRET
ICE SKATING

Once winter settles on Boston Common, the only signs of amphibian life at **Frog Pond** (Boston Common, near Beacon Street, 617-635-2120) are the strains of "Jeremiah Was a Bullfrog" wafting out of the hi-fi system. A man-made ice-skating rink of modest dimensions in the heart of Boston's oldest park, Frog Pond is no Rockefeller Center. With its '70s nostalgia music, snack shack, and park benches, Frog Pond is more like a neighborhood rink. But its neighborhood is all of Boston. On weekdays, office workers whip out their passes to spend a carefree lunch hour circling under snowy trees. School holidays find scores of ankle-biters scooting round the rink, breaking only for a hot chocolate when the Zamboni revs its motor and chugs out to polish the ice. It's at night, however, when city lights sparkle and the stars wink down, that this urban rink shines. Whether you can skate or not, it's one of the city's best dates: for skaters, it's as good as a tango. For non-skaters, the sport provides all the necessary excuses to tumble into the arms of their lovies.

Ice skating begins in November and lasts through mid-March (call for a schedule). The price is $3 for skaters aged 14 and over, free for 13 and under. Rentals of figure and hockey skates are $5. Ask about season's and lunchtime passes and about figure skating instruction for ages three to adult.

S E C R E T

INDIAN

✼

The name, **Gourmet India** (1335 Beacon Street, Brookline, 617-734-3971) implies the kind of white-linen Indian restaurant that has become so trendy of late, but this new Brookline eatery is as casual as a sandwich shop, with prices to match. It's the North Indian fare — expertly prepared and very fresh — that earns the name "gourmet." Main dishes are served buffet style, so you can inspect the offerings before selecting from meat dishes like kebabs and korma (chicken with nuts and raisins in a cream sauce) or vegetarian meals like saag paneer (spinach and cheese) served with a side of aromatic basmati rice. But don't overlook the nan (flat bread). Variations include mint nan, garlic and cilantro nan, chicken nan, and the exotic Peshwari nan layered with dried fruits and coconut. You know it's fresh because you can watch the baker pull it hot from the tandoori oven. If you're

in a hurry, pop in for a quick samosa (two for $1.95). These Indian bus-stop snacks are made from potatoes, peas, and spices and deep-fried in a light pastry wrapping. Or try one of the roll-ups: lamb or chicken stuffed into one of those freshly baked nan.

The proprietor of **Thar Treasures** (55 South Street, 617-983-4090) has provisioned his JP boutique with the textiles, furniture, music, jewelry, and art of his home state of Rajasthan — an area of north-west India noted for its fine handicrafts. Both new and antique imports pack the shop, from centuries-old carved granary doors con-verted into cabinets ($1400) to smaller items like brightly painted wooden cabinets depicting Indian paramours. Intensely colored tex-tiles form treasure-hunt piles here and there throughout the shop. Antique embroidered wall hangings are exquisite (and pricey), but there are also less expensive new embroidered and mirrored textiles (pillow covers, bedspreads, curtains) with less detailed workmanship, but no less charm. Look also for paintings on silk and wood, reams of sari silk, and bronze statuettes of the pantheon of Indian gods. On Newbury Street, **India Antiques** (279 Newbury Street, 617-266-6539) specializes in henna decorations for your hands and feet, as well as fine silver jewelry, antique fabric stamps, figurines, and textiles.

Now playing: *Raju Chacha*, starring Ajay Devgan, Kajol, and Rishi Kapoor, directed by Anil Devgan. That's the hit of the week in the world of Bollywood, the Indian equivalent of Hollywood. Scores of feature films are produced in Mumbai (formerly Bombay) each year. Arlington's **Bombay Cinema** (Regent Theater, 7 Medford Street, Arlington, 978-671-9212, 781-643-1198, www.aapkamanoranjan. com) screens these first-run films and sponsors live events. Samosas are for sale in the lobby during intermission.

SECRET
INDUSTRIAL HISTORY

"Walk in there and tell me where you think you are," says Bruce Whetle of Arlington's **Old Schwamb Mill** (17 Mill Lane, off Lowell Street, 781-643-0554). The mill smells of dried wood and machine oil. Giant fan belts, wheels, and pulleys stand idle overhead, and the floor is covered in sawdust and wood shavings. Rough hand tools lie on oak worktables and antique jigsaws gleam next to oval lathes. "Um. They made elliptical picture frames?" I surmise. "Not made: *make*," corrects Bruce. Old Schwamb Mill, it turns out, is more than a museum. It's a working, 19th-century oval frame factory.

While mills have occupied this spot for more than 350 years, the current buildings date from 1864. Once run on waterpower, the mill is now electrified, but the lathes are still pulley driven. In the office, which also hasn't changed its 19th-century mien — with its rolltop desk and iron vault lettered "Clinton W. Schwamb Co" — there's a picture of the Schwamb clan outside their mill in 1873. The family ran the mill for five generations, but by the 1960s the rise of plastic-injection molding and metal frames caused the Schwambs to sell. Rather than see the old mill demolished, a group of Arlington volunteers formed a nonprofit trust to preserve this relic of the Industrial Revolution. The mill is open Tuesdays (2 PM to 4 PM) or by appointment; call for information about admission fees. During visits, the turner David Graf walks visitors through the whole process, showing how he measures, cuts, and finishes a frame.

Waltham's sobriquet, "Watch City," derives from its once proud watchmaking industry, one of several manufacturing concerns remem-

bered at the **Charles River Museum of Industry** (154 Moody
Street, Waltham, 781-893-5410). The museum traces this Boston
neighbor's history as one of the birthplaces of the Industrial Revolution. America's first power looms were built in these restored Francis
Cabot Lowell mill buildings. The oldest of the buildings was erected
in 1814, and the manufacturing systems that developed here inspired
the building of other early New England textile cities, such as Lowell
(where the Merrimack River provided 20 times more power than the
Charles). Today, the converted Waltham mills house artists' studios,
residences, and light manufacturing and commercial space, while the
museum occupies the former powerhouse with its gigantic smokestack.

While the Charles River Museum of Industry's exhibits are somewhat haphazard, anyone with a love for how things work or an eye
for industrial architecture will find happiness here. In the watch
display, enamel faceplates tout defunct businesses, and cases hold tiny
metal lathes, a watchmaker's bench, 20th-century alarm clocks, punch
clocks, player piano parts, and pocket watches. Downstairs in the
massive engine room, there's an 1871 steam fire engine, and a 1907
Orient Runabout, representing the story of auto manufacturing in
Greater Boston. In the early 20th century, there were three auto
plants along the Charles River: Waltham had the Waltham Manufacturing Company (later Metz Auto). In Newton it was the Stanley
Steamer Company, and in Cambridge the Ford Model T plant. By the
1920s, these plants were all but gone. Ford had outpaced them all by
introducing mass production and heading for the Midwest, where
production costs were lower and suburban markets enormous. Open
Monday to Saturday (10 AM to 5 PM) and by appointment; $4.

Farther afield, the story of the Industrial Revolution reaches back to
its colonial roots at the **Saugus Iron Works National Historic Site**

(244 Central Street, Saugus, 781-233-0050), a 17th-century reconstruction. Open daily with weekend tours. The fascinating **Lowell
National Historical Park** (visitors' center, 246 Market Street, 978-
970-5000) commemorates the nation's first full-fledged industrial city
at the Boott Cotton Mills Museum.

S E C R E T
INLINE SKATING

The paved bikeways profiled under "Secret Cycling" are perfect for
inline skating, especially the uncrowded Southwest Corridor Linear
Park. Also of note for bladers are the following: on Sundays (11 AM
to 7 PM) from April to November, Memorial Drive from Western Ave
to the Eliot Bridge (Harvard Square) is closed to traffic. In Roxbury,
Franklin Park has 4.5 miles of paved paths. A track through the Back
Bay Fens from Fenway Drive and Brookline Avenue runs past the
Museum of Fine Arts and then back along Park Avenue to Brookline
Avenue for a two-mile loop. Brighton's **Chestnut Hill Reservoir**
has a 1.5-mile course with views of the reservoir and Boston College.
A spectacular 2.1-mile paved ring surrounds **Pleasure Bay** in South
Boston.

If you want company, join one of the many events of the **Inline
Club of Boston** (781-932-5457, www.icbskates.org). During the
warm months, the club sponsors group slaloms for a variety of skill
levels. On Tuesdays (7 PM), intermediate skaters meet at the Hatch
Memorial Shell on the Charles River Esplanade; every Sunday (10:15
AM), "until it snows," beginning to intermediate bladers take off from

JFK Park (Memorial Drive, Cambridge). Call for additional meeting places, times, and events.

S E C R E T

INNER PEACE

At the **Cambridge Insight Meditation Center** (331 Broadway, Cambridge, 617-441-9038, 617-491-5070), one learns that meditation is much more than a stress reduction technique. In fact, getting de-stressed is a by-product of a process of lifelong learning that can be sparked by the simple act of sitting down and "paying attention to your breath." Of the several meditation centers in Greater Boston, CIMC is probably the least intimidating for Westerners and newcomers to the art of meditation. There's a drop-in class on Tuesday nights with a half-hour of sitting, as well as a short walking meditation, followed by a question and answer session with one of the center's senior teachers. All are welcome. (Tip: wear clean socks.) Each Wednesday, all are invited to help with housecleaning (excellent for your karma), followed by 45 minutes of sitting and a dharma talk ("dharma" can be translated, roughly, as seeing the way things really are), applying Buddhist philosophy to subjects from world peace to intimate relationships. It's all very low key. You walk, you sit, you talk. "That's about as exciting as things get around here," says Narayan Leibenson Grady, one of the teachers. Call for a brochure, which describes ongoing programs, events, and guest speakers.

There are several other area meditation centers to consider. The **Zen Center of Cambridge** (199 Auburn Street, Cambridge, 617-576-3229) has a walk-in introductory session each Monday evening

(7 PM). **Boston Shambhala Center** (646 Brookline Avenue, Brookline, 617-734-1498) hosts a variety of programs that are open to the public. The **International Buddhist Progress Society** (950 Massachusetts Avenue, Cambridge, 617-547-6670) offers meditation, as well as courses in tai chi, Chinese language, painting, sculpture, the art of Chinese knots, and vegetarian cooking. There's a little tearoom here, too, with vegetarian snacks like steamed dumplings on the menu. The gift shop sells books on Buddhism and "alter supplies."

S E C R E T

IRISH

Since the beginning of the 20th century, the Irish have been Boston's largest ethnic group. They now make up about 20 percent of the total population of Bostonian and Irish immigration continues unabated. You're nearly as likely to hear an Irish accent as a Boston one, especially if you're talking to a bartender.

A host of Irish pubs serve beer you could eat with a spoon and Irish music from the ancient to the new wave. In traditional "seissuns," players do their thing purely for their own satisfaction, typically seated in a semi-circle with an ale at their elbow. Anyone's welcome to listen and tap toes. One of the best places to do that is the **Burren** (247 Elm Street, Somerville, 617-776-6896), where seissuns take place in the front room (while plugged-in bands are booked for the back) every night of the week.

Because seissuns favor playing over singing, Dublin-born musician Seamus Walker founded the **Boston Folk & Traditional Singers Club**, where Celtic and other traditional and ballad-style singing gets a joyous airing each Wednesday (9:30 PM) from autumn to spring. The singers meet in a third-floor room at **Paddy Burke's** (132 Portland Street, at Merrimac Street). Both singers and listeners are warmly welcomed. For details contact Seamus Walker (978-546-6409).

Most of Boston's Irish pubs serve decent food, but something special goes on at **James's Gate** (5–11 McBride Street, at South Street, 617-983-2000). On the pub side of this dual establishment, a roaring fire warms the room, while ales and light fare are served up from the polished bar. On the restaurant side, the menu roams the globe, landing on dishes like pepper-crusted tuna with wasabi sauce or crab-stuffed halibut in a leek-tomato reduction. The fare is seasonal; on a hot summer night, I've enjoyed a cooling cucumber and avocado soup with a peppery bite. But before you start, order a pint or half pint of Guinness to go with the warm crusty bread and black olives that come to your table unbidden. On the tail end of dinner, dessert might be the "granny," a slice of moist apple cake drizzled with caramel and topped with crème fraîche. Main courses range from $6 to $20.

Irish culture is not all Guinness-guzzling and fiddling. The Irish are known for their magical way with the written (and spoken) word. Each year, the **Bloomsday Players** (617-929-0283) celebrate the fictional Dubliner Leopold Bloom with dramatic readings from James Joyce's *Ulysses*. The event takes place on Boston Common at 5 PM on Bloomsday, June 16 — the day that Joyce's *Ulysses* takes place.

Rambling through the North End, Back Bay, and Beacon Hill, the three-mile-long **Irish Heritage Trail** (Boston Irish Tourism Association, 20 Buckingham Road, Milton, 617-696-9880, www.irishheritagetrail.com) is a self-guided tour unearthing the tales of Boston's Irish politicians, artists, and heroes. For more on Irish cultural tourism in Boston, contact the **Boston Irish Tourism Association** (www.irishmassachusetts.com).

JAPANESE

With a Japanese grocery store, a Japanese art and gift shop, any number of sushi and noodle eateries, and even a Franco-Japanese pastry shop, **Porter Exchange** shopping mall (1815 Massachusetts Avenue) is Greater Boston's Little Tokyo. Most of the dining establishments here are no bigger than stalls, set side by side in an alley-like hall. Walk down the strip and browse the menus. The tables are usually packed with Japanese students discussing pop culture over a bowl of noodles. **Tampopo** (617-868-5457) — recalling the zany movie of the same name — does lovely noodles. Their fat udons topped with lightly battered tempura of shrimp, sweet potatoes, and green beans are sublime sprinkled with a little shichimi togarashi, a spice made from red pepper, sesame seeds, seaweed, orange peel, and mulberry. One of mankind's greatest inventions, the sushi bar, is represented by **Kotobukiya** (617-492-5330). Like any worthwhile sushi bar, the tone is casual while the food and preparation are rigorously orchestrated. Kotobukiya runs a grocery store around the corner (still in Porter Exchange, 617-354-6914) with sliced and wrapped choice bits of yellowfin, octopus, and squid in the deli case for make-your-own sushi. The store has a wall of Japanese movies and television dramas for rent, as well as hair products, pottery, magazines, and more. **Japonaise** (617-547-5531) does French-style pastries with a Far East twist: green tea cheese cake, puff pastry filled with adzuki bean paste, and curry rolls, as well as dainty finger sandwiches for lunching, and sweet and savory croissants. Finally, **Tokai** (617-864-5922) carries Japanese pottery, origami papers, vintage kimonos, colorful carp windsocks ($1.50 to $18), kitsch "good fortune" cats, printed rice papers, and items for all your *feng shui* needs (tinkling fountains, incense, candles). The store has another location on Newbury Street (207 Newbury Street, 617-578-0976).

Across Mass Ave from Porter Exchange, **Sasuga Japanese Bookstore** (7 Upland Road, Cambridge, 617-497-5460) has books, magazines, and comics, as well as a few English titles about Japan.

A Japanese Buddhist-inspired celebration takes place at Forest Hills Cemetery each July. The annual **Lantern Festival** (95 Forest Hills Avenue, Jamaica Plain, 617-524-0128), not to be confused with the Lantern Parade (see "Secret Emerald Necklace"), features Japanese music, dance, and taiko drumming. The event ends with a remembrance ceremony, when participants decorate and inscribe messages of peace on lanterns, lighting them and floating them at twilight on Lake Hibiscus. Bring a picnic.

SECRET

JAZZ AND BLUES

Boston's free-form jazz groups offer a steady diet of unpredictability. For an eon or so, the eight-plus members of the **Bad Art Ensemble** have been doing a weekly-gig at the Plough & Stars (912 Massachusetts Avenue, Cambridge, 617-441-3455) featuring, as the they put it, "a Brechtian songbook of bittersweet delights with irreverent American music from Dixieland to Jazz and Pop." More improvised jazz can be found at **Zeitgeist Gallery** (312 Broadway, at Norfolk Street, Cambridge, 617-876-2182), which hosts the North Beach-inspired

Subconscious Café a couple of times a month, as well as other improv events, some of which also feature dance and video. Once a week, the **Lizard Lounge** (1667 Massachusetts Avenue, at Harvard Street, Cambridge, 617-547-0759) turns over the stage to the Fringe, another long-running free-jazz combo. Look up the Web site of **Boston Improv** (members.aol.com/tautology3/BossImpCal.html) for all the happenings.

The main fare at high-flying **Scullers** (Doubletree Suites, 400 Soldiers Field Road, at River Street, 617-783-0090, 617-562-4111), as well as at the somewhat more reasonably priced **Regattabar** (Charles Hotel, 1 Bennett Street, Cambridge, 617-661-5000), is world-class jazz, blues, Latin, R&B, and soul. Ticket prices at these glitzy hotel cocktail lounge clubs can run as high as $30. But seeing jazz live doesn't have to be expensive. **Ryles** (212 Hampshire Street, Cambridge, 617-876-9330) charges cheaper covers, showcasing jazz from near and far in its laid-back rooms. **Wally's** (427 Massachusetts Avenue, 617-424-1408) is a jazz legend. This hole-in-the-wall club has been vibrating to blues, Latin jazz, and fusion since 1947. Not to be confused with Boston Improv (above), there is smoke-free jazz at **ImprovBoston** (Back Alley Theatre, 1253 Cambridge Street, Cambridge, 617-576-1253) every Thursday night (9 PM); $9.

Weekly blues jams ("bringing your ax") happen at **Johnny D's** (17 Holland Street, Somerville, 617-776-2004), the **Cantab Lounge** (738 Massachusetts Avenue, Cambridge, 617-354-2685), Wally's (above), and the **Midway Café** (3496 Washington Street, Jamaica Plain, 617-524-9038). Major blues venues are the **House of Blues** (96 Winthrop Street, 617-491-2583), Ryles (above), and Scullers (above). The **Boston Blues Society** (8 Plympton Street, Cambridge, 617-876-2583) has all the grit at its Web site (www.bostonblues.com).

SECRET
KIDS' MUSEUMS

Boston's four-story **Children's Museum** (300 Congress Street, 617-426-8855), set in a former warehouse along Museum Wharf, was one of the country's first museums to cater specially to kids. It's a great museum, endowed not only with zillions of things to push, pull, build, and climb on, but with a social conscience as well. It's also endowed with big crowds. Open daily (10 AM to 5 PM, and until 9 PM on Fridays). Normally admission is $7 for adults and $6 for children, but on Friday evenings (5 PM to 9 PM) admission is $1 per person.

But, guess what? When Boston parents want to have a blast with their kids, they don't necessarily head for Congress Street. Many of them have found the short drive to the 'burbs to visit the **Discovery Museums** (177 Main Street, Acton, 978-264-4200) well worth their while. Situated in a shady grove along Route 27 in Acton (look for the green stegosaurus, one mile south of Route 2), this pair of museums — the Children's and the Science Discovery Museums — present the most intriguing and whimsical children's exhibits in the region. Set in a rambling Victorian, the Children's Discovery Museum is made for kids up to age four. When I visited with a couple of pint-sized companions, it felt more like a trip to grandma's house than a formal outing. We commenced with the dinosaur room, where we took apart and reassembled a near-life-sized wooden dino skeleton. Next, the "chain reaction" room kept us captivated for the better part of an hour with its Goldbergesque maze where the kids (okay! I admit it, I hogged) sent rubber balls down see-through tubes to knock down lines of blocks, launch a parachute, or make a gong go bing, bang, bong. When the littler of my pals got tired of the hubbub, he

found a cozy nest in the old hearth that's been turned into a cushioned reading nook. Then, we "swam" upstairs (the stairwell is painted to give the illusion of the deep sea). There, we found Bessie's Diner mobbed with wannabe chefs serving play food to patient parents, so we moved on to the Forest Room, where we dressed up as bluebirds and slid down hollow tree trunks.

Next door at the Science Discovery Museum, a couple of school-aged girls were creating a "mist tornado." Five cents gave us the privilege of making our own giant Spirograph drawing. While my friends stared in awe as their artwork developed before their eyes, I wandered into the "inventor's workshop," where older girls in safety goggles lined a workbench banging nails into wood. Hovering over the would-be carpenters was a bevy of anxious dads coaching them on how to get a "good hit."

While the Discovery Museums are off the beaten track, they are exceedingly well patronized by those in the know. Museum staff will never let the crowds get so overwhelming that kids can't enjoy themselves. That means that when the museums reach capacity, a waiting list begins. Parking becomes tight well before that point. The quietest time to visit is after noon, especially on Wednesdays, when the museums stay open later. Call for hours; $7 for one museum, $10 for both.

SECRET

KOREAN

The menu at **Suishaya** (57 Beach Street, 617-423-3889), a cozy Korean place in the heart of Chinatown, ranges far beyond the staple kimchi (cabbage mixed with various spices) dishes. I like the orderliness of the "box lunches." Order one and a square enamel serving dish with compartments neatly dividing your courses will arrive at your table. I sampled the chicken bulgaki, with tender chunks of meat and sautéed vegetables marinated in a spicy Korean-style sauce and hints of sesame and tomato. Tucked away beside it were big bites of vegetable and shrimp tempura, miso soup, and salad.

Another capital Korean place is **Seoul Food** (1759 Massachusetts Avenue, 617-864-6299), a hole-in-the-wall serving vegetable pancakes, a cross between an omelette and a pizza, doused with vinegar and soy sauce. Also recommended: seaweed salad, bibim-baps (beef, veggie, chicken, or tofu), or spiced pork bulgaki stir-fried with broccoli. Open daily (10 AM to 10 PM).

In Union Square, the **Reliable Market** (45 Union Square, Somerville, 617-623-9620) stocks Korean ingredients and ready-mades. It's a pleasure to browse the orderly aisles here, if for no other reason than to enjoy the designer packaging, or to try to imagine what you'd do with an entire school of whole, dried anchovies. Before you check out, consider adding a tub of California-made adzuki bean-flavored ice cream to your shopping basket.

SECRET
LATIN DANCE

On full moon nights in summer, a metamorphosis takes place on the Weeks Footbridge (Harvard Square), when the **Tango Society of Boston** (617-699-6246) commandeers the little stone arch over the

Charles for **Tango by Moonlight** (Metropolitan District Commission, 617-699-6246). Like a chiaroscuro painting, the scene unfolds, as dancers glide, pause, and move across the pavement — their pinned-together bodies creating long, eerie shadows. Argentine music floats out over the water, a small crowd watches, people weave through the congregation looking for a partner. These moonlight dances have been a fixture on the Weeks Footbridge for five years, but very few people know about them. The instruction is informal; there's no "okay everybody, a one, a two, a three." Mini-lessons sometimes take place, but if you want to learn, your best bet is to find one of the instructors and ask. The dance begins at 8 PM and runs until 11 PM; free. You might want to get a head start with the society's weekly introductory **tango lesson**, which takes place every Wednesday (7:30 PM to 11:30 PM) at the VFW Mt. Auburn Post (688 Huron Avenue, Cambridge, 617-699-6246). Lessons run from 7:30 PM to 8:30 PM, followed by dancing from 8:30 PM to 11:30 PM; $5.

Tango, samba, bossa nova, merengue, salsa. It's all Latin dance, and it's all over Boston. Almost every club in the city has at least one night devoted to one or more of these dance forms, but the best are the smaller clubs where live bands turn up the heat. Among those offering lessons and live music are **Johnny D's** (17 Holland Street, Somerville, 617-776-2004); **Ryles** (212 Hampshire Street, Cambridge, 617-876-9330); the **Milky Way Lounge & Lanes** (403–405 Centre Street, 617-524-3740); the **Jorge Hernandez Cultural Center** (65 West Newton Street, 617-867-9191); and **Club Juliana** (above the New Lei Jing Seafood Restaurant, third floor, 20 Hudson Street, at Kneeland Street, 617-354-5780). There is as well the very sophisticated **Sophia's** (1270 Boylston Street, 617-351-7001), a tapas bar/nightclub with rooftop salsa in the summer and various Latin happenings on several floors throughout the year, including salsa and merengue lessons, and a live jazzy salsa band. Open Thursday to Saturday (9 PM to 1 AM). Go early to avoid the lines.

For the complete up-to-the-minute story on Latin dance in Boston, contact **Salsa Boston** (617-513-9841, www.salsaboston.com).

S E C R E T

LODGING

Picture this: for $90, two people can stay at a ship-shape, waterfront bed and breakfast, complete with a splash pool, gas grills, and unparalleled city views, right on the Freedom Trail.

There are, however, a few catches. First, there's no electricity (but there is running water and a toilet). Second, your "room" is about five by eight feet wide. But that's because your accommodation is a snug little sailboat called the *Maine Course.* Docked at Constitution Marina, this 24-foot O'Day is the smallest of the sail-, house-, and motor-boats in the marina's **B&B Afloat** fleet (Constitution Marina, 28 Constitution Road, 617-241-9640). Bob Navin, the charter manager at Constitution Marina, says of the *Maine Course,* "It's camping," and admits they don't get many calls for the little boat. Many more guests decide to pretend they're The Donald for a night and rent the *Rozinante* ($300), a luxury yacht complete with a two-person Jacuzzi and a DVD player, or *My Holiday* ($275), a 50-foot motor cruiser with a leather-upholstered living room set, two bedrooms, and a washer and dryer. Then there is *Clear Day,* a 46-foot sailboat with acres of glossy teak, blue velvet upholstery, and a snug U-shaped deck where guests can watch the stars come out over the twinkling Boston sky-line. For those who want the adventure of sleeping afloat without the minor inconveniences of a yacht, the marina provides the purpose-built *Port & Starboard,* a pontoon houseboat. Once inside, you'd be hard pressed to distinguish your room from a nice, standard motel room — if it weren't for the occasional gentle bobbing.

Whether you decide to "camp" on the *Maine Course* or camp it up in *My Holiday,* the location of this floating B&B could hardly be better. Home to 300 handsome boats, the marina is right on the Freedom Trail and next to the Charlestown Navy Yard (home of "Old Ironsides"). Guests often walk up for the sunset flag lowering and cannon salute. A short walk over the bridge is the North End, with its endless dining and sightseeing, and Charlestown (think Bunker Hill) is at your doorstep — or, rather, deck step. The friendly marina staff delivers a continental breakfast to you on the boat. For other meals, you can cook on gas grills by the pleasant little pool at the flower-decked marina office.

If you're not camping on a sailboat, you're very likely going to pay dearly for a hotel room in Boston. So as long as you're splurging, consider one of Beacon Hill's new, small hotels.

Let's say it right up front: a night at the 61-room **XV Beacon Hotel** (15 Beacon Street, 617-670-1500) will set you back around $595. A Founding Fathers theme (busts, patriotic etchings, and even a couple of Gilbert Stuart portraits) predominates throughout this strenuously orchestrated hotel. Gas fireplaces and all sorts of bells and whistles (high-speed Internet hook-ups, fax machines) — as well as bathrooms with oversized showerheads that deliver a cataract of water, heated towel racks, and whirlpools — make the rooms pretty well earn the term luxurious, though spacious they are not. The room rate includes a free in-town sedan service; you won't find XV patrons hailing a cab. **The Federalist** restaurant has an award-winning bartender, but its big boast is its *Wine Spectator*-feted cellar of 25,000 bottles.

Less than two years old, the smaller **Beacon Hill Hotel & Bistro** (19 Charles Street, 617-723-7575, 888-959-2442) has 12 rooms and one small suite atop the eponymous bistro, which serves French food priced, as owner Cecelia Rait points out, "very reasonably for Boston." The hotel lobby *is* the restaurant, so don't look for a place to sit here, unless you want to be handed a menu. But once you see the rooms, it's apparent that equal care and attention goes into both sides of the business. Upstairs from the narrow dining room with its smart, minimal décor, the small guestrooms are decorated in earthy colors, with charming views of Charles Street. The hotel is set in two mid-19th-century brick buildings, and a breezeway on an upper floor connecting the buildings has been set up as a very pleasant terrace. A full breakfast in the bistro is included in the room rates, which range from $225 to $345.

A third Beacon Hill newcomer is the two-year-old **Charles Street Inn** (94 Charles Street, 617-314-8900, 877-772-8900), with nine rooms named after local celebrities of the Victorian era. Rooms here are spacious and stuffed with turn-of-the-century antiques and Oriental throw rugs; handsome armoires stand in for closets. There are marble fireplaces, as well as contemporary comforts like a whirlpool and two phone lines. The rooms with queen beds have better views and more sunlight, but there are no duds here. While the Ralph Waldo Emerson is the grandest, I favor the Isabella Stewart Gardner, with its swell-front window, impossibly high ceilings, narrow doors, wood-burning fireplace, and chandelier. The staff brings continental breakfast to your room each morning. This small hotel is often booked up from August to October, so try to reserve a month in advance during peak times. Prices range from $280 to $340.

If you're planning on exploring MIT's and Harvard's great museums (see "Secret Art," Secret Technology," and "Secret Harvard"), staying in Cambridge will put you the center of the action. The four-year-old **University Park Hotel@MIT** (20 Sidney Street, Cambridge, 617-577-0200, 800-222-8733) has received a lot of press for its high-tech design, which might lead you to expect a certain stark industrial chic at this Central Square hotel. But the designers have done a nice job of humanizing the spaces while incorporating themes from science and technology — like the giant molecule carpet. Rooms are standard issue but include decorating touches that add a comforting sense of place: dressers with inlaid circuit boards, grainy black-and-white photographs of MIT bigwigs and feats in history. The hotel stands out, however, for its flourishing rooftop garden, with Adirondack chairs and a stone fountain. Prices start at around $200. The restaurant, Sidney's Grille (617-494-0011), serves moderately priced "eclectic American." Meanwhile, "quiet elegance" is the theme at the **Inn at Harvard** (1201 Massachusetts Avenue, Cambridge, 617-491-2222, 800-458-5886), where high tea is served six days a week (see "Secret Tea").

S E C R E T
LOST GARDEN

Longtime home of the star-crossed Boston Celtics basketball team, the **Boston Garden** was demolished a few years back to make room for the hangar-like Fleet Center. The Celtics, who've won more championships than any other NBA team, are rather on the skids these days. Maybe it's the curse of the Boston Garden. In any case, the beloved Garden now lives on only in memory at the Arsenal Mall

(485 Arsenal Street, Watertown, 617-923-4700), where the former mall owner is reported to have paid $40,000 for the Boston Garden **scoreboard**. See it in the second-floor food court. Also, interested parties can purchase a chunk of the old Garden parquet floor or a couple of creaky wooden seats — at least, while they last (www. fleetcenter.com/store).

S E C R E T
MARATHONERS

The **Boston Marathon** was first run in 1897 with 16 competitors. Today, nearly 18,000 official runners and uncounted "bandits," as the Boston Athletic Association (BAA) has dubbed unofficial runners, make the 26.2-mile charge from the town of Hopkinton to **Copley Square.** Official top finishers in all divisions compete for prize money totaling $525,000.

The country's oldest marathon, Boston's stature in the world of long-distance runners is based on its exclusivity. In order to enter the race with a number, you must run a "qualifying time" (the Boston Marathon Web site, www.bostonmarathon.org, lists times for all divisions) at a certified marathon during the winter preceding the Boston Marathon. Boston is the only marathon, other than the Olympics, that requires this.

Still, lots of numberless runners go for it each year. The BAA doesn't kick these back-of-the-packers off the course. They just frown vigorously on them, complaining that they sap resources from more deserving competitors. But many see the unofficial runners as a part of the grassroots spirit of the Boston Marathon, and no one disputes that they are just as committed to the grueling task of getting to Copley Square as those wearing numbers.

S E C R E T

MEDITERRANEAN

I love the aromatic, fruit-and-grain-laced cuisines of the Mediterranean. Here are three Greater Boston restaurants serving the heavenly cuisines of north Africa and southern Europe at down-to-earth prices.

Once in a while you stumble across a restaurant that gets everything right: atmosphere, service, food, value. **Baraka Café** (80 Pearl Street, Cambridgeport, 617-868-3951) is such a place. There's no sign out front. Head down Pearl Street from Central Square and look for the blue awning on the left. With just four tables and a handful of booths, this tiny north African restaurant makes the most of its space, with colored glass globes suspended from the ceiling, an exposed brick wall, and subdued lighting. The Algerian and Tunisian fare created by chef Krimo Dahim is so varied and fascinating that by the time you leave, you may already be looking forward to your next visit. Try starting with the karentika, a custard made of chickpeas served with harrissa tapenade, then move on to a traditional couscous — light and mild, with a nicely spiced bouillon of vegetables, lentils, chickpeas, and fava beans. Or create a meal of mezzes. Like tapas, these small plates can be combined for mix-and-match nibbling — great for sharing around the table, they're so good you may want to hoard them. Along with the mezzes, it's essential to order bread such as zatar, a zesty grilled Berber bread spiced with wild thyme, sage, and sesame seeds. Baraka is not widely known, but it does have a loyal following and can get crowded on weekend nights, so arrive early or be prepared for a short wait.

Restaurateur brothers George and Themis Boretos run a tight ship. Take a seat at their North Cambridge place, **Greek Corner** (2366 Massachusetts Avenue, Cambridge, 617-661-5655), and your waitress is usually ready to take your order before your chair gets warm. Once you've placed your order from the lengthy menu, there's precious little time to take in your surroundings before your meal arrives, so I'll sum it up for you: a sunny dining area decorated with Mediterranean dream murals backed by the tinkling sounds of balalaika. In addition to arriving with arresting alacrity, the food here is the best Greek in the region. I'm partial to the gyros. Greek Corner prepares them not only with the traditional spiced lamb, but also as a chicken or vegetarian dish. Any way you take them, the gyros have just the right combination of tangy onions, creamy sauce, and herbs nestled in fresh bread. Have one with a side of Greek fries, cooked in the skin and served sprinkled with feta, oregano, and a dash of lemon juice.

Author of the *Sultan's Kitchen* cookbook, chef-owner Özcan Ozan has presided over his Financial District restaurant of the same name for nearly two decades now. At **Sultan's Kitchen** (72 Broad Street, 617-728-2828), Ozan does Turkish food like tangy lemon chicken soup; tender swordfish kebabs with a side of rice, feta, and salad; or chicken durum, a blend of grilled chicken with roasted red peppers and eggplant. Lunchtime usually finds a line strung out onto Broad Street from the counter on the lower floor of this old brick building. But the staff is so efficient that the line always moves fast. In summer I like to take my baba ganoush (roasted eggplant with garlic) up to Post Office Square and sprawl on the grass with the office workers.

But if you don't want to schlep, there's a pleasant eating area upstairs. For years strictly a lunch place, Mr. Ozan's kitchen is now open until 8 PM for carry-out — much to the delight of downtowners, who can now not only have their lunch here but can also bring dinner home.

S E C R E T

MIDNIGHT RIDE

"Listen my child and you shall hear of the midnight ride of Paul Revere." We all know Henry Wadsworth Longfellow's story of the events of April 18 and 19, 1775: Patriot Paul Revere slipped across the river to Charlestown, borrowed a horse, and waited for his accomplice to light a lantern or two in the steeple of the Old North Church. Then off he sped to warn the Minutemen at Lexington and Concord, 60 miles out of Boston, of the approaching British regulars.

What most people don't realize is that Longfellow's retelling of events that led to the start of the American Revolution was built largely on poetic license. The poet laureate writes of Revere, "It was two by the village clock, when he came to the bridge in Concord town." But the silversmith never made it to Concord. He was captured just outside Lexington. Another rider, William Dawes, whose route had taken him through Roxbury and Brookline, managed to escape the British patrols but had to turn back short of his goal in order to avoid capture. A third horseman, 29-year-old Dr. Samuel Prescott, joined the race in Lexington, where he had been calling on his girl-friend, Lydia Mulliken. Apparently, Miss Mulliken's father had thrown the suitor out of the house, and it was that event that precipitated the chance meeting with the other riders. Prescott managed to

evade the British and continue to Concord and beyond. I suppose "The Midnight Ride of Dr. Samuel Prescott" just didn't fit the meter.

One of the unassailable stars of the tale, however, is the **Old North Church** (195 Salem Street, 617-723-7160), the place where the lanterns were hung on that fateful night. Boston's oldest church is also noted for its supporting role in the adventures of John Childe, who in 1757 flew successfully from the Old North's steeple — three times. The Old North is a bright light on the Freedom Trail. If you care to visit, there's a 50-minute guided tour that takes in the church, colonial garden, and bell tower (June to October; $8). From July to October on Thursday and Friday nights (8 PM), an actor dons the role of Paul Revere to tell the story of his life, from his participation in the Boston Tea Party to his role as a forensic dentist in the Battle of Bunker Hill. Tickets are $12.

The **lantern** hung in the Old North Church steeple on the night of the famous ride is among the collection at the Concord Museum (200 Lexington Road, Concord, 978-369-5477). And the **grave of Robert Newton**, the sexton of the Old North Church who sent the famous signal to Revere, can be visited at Copp's Hill Burying Ground (see "Secret Cemeteries").

S E C R E T

MIT FLEA

One of the largest electronics "swapfests" in New England, the MIT **Flea** (Albany and Main streets, Cambridge, 617-253-3776) has been in operation for nearly 20 years. Every third Sunday from April to October (9 AM to 2 PM; $5), some 200 vendors show up, filling the

Albany Street Garage and spilling into the adjacent parking lot. On offer: industrial surplus, electronic components, computer servers, lab equipment, radios, microscopes — in short, everything under the technological sun. From the latest computer software to a working World War II voltage meter, the dealers have seen it and sold it. "There is no limit," says one. "If it's electronic, sooner or later it will wind up here." The prices run the gamut, too. "I don't forget the $2 stuff," says another merchant as he inspects a shrink-wrapping machine a colleague is selling. "You need that, man," says the colleague. Even among each other, these guys are hagglers.

The mastermind behind the sale is cowboy hat-wearing Steve Finberg, who says around 1,000 potential buyers show up each month for the sale, which attracts both technophiles and artists. In fact, one of the groups that sponsors the swapfest, the MIT Electronics Research Society, has a regular "potluck, show-and-tell, performance art night" the Friday before the flea (MIT Museum Building, Room N52-115, 265 Massachusetts Avenue, Cambridge, 617-253-2060), when just about anything can happen, and does.

S E C R E T
MONEY

It's an Old Money town, so you might expect Boston's government bank to be a granite pile, squatting toad-like in a dim courtyard spattered with pigeon dung. No so. The **Federal Reserve Bank of Boston** (Educational Programs and Tours, 600 Atlantic Avenue, 617-973-3464) is 32 sleek stories of glass and steel located next to busy South station. One of 12 reserve banks in the United States, Boston's fed doesn't print money (that's done in DC at the Bureau of Engraving and Printing). Instead, the bank merrily shreds it; some $10 million worth of worn-out currency gets turned into coleslaw here every day. Tours of the fed will get you up to speed on the concept of central banking (I must admit, that one has kept me awake nights). For one thing, before President Wilson put the Federal Reserve System in place in 1913, any organization could print money; at one time there were 30,000 varieties in circulation, a situation that raised havoc with banks' ability to determine whether currency was genuine. Even with the new United States currency's sophisticated anti-counterfeiting features, a large part of what the Fed does today is to make sure the counterfeit buck stops here.

Unlike New York's fed, Boston's has no gold in its vaults, just $3 billion in cash. Your guide will take you around to see bricks of it being sorted, weighed, and, of course, shredded. And there's a nifty video narrated by a bow-tied Charles Osgood in which you'll learn how the fed keeps the United States economy stable by buying and selling government bonds, thus adding and subtracting money from the nation's supply. Whatever!

Be sure to stick around at the end of the tour for your free sample of genuine United States currency... shredded. The 90-minute tour takes place on the first and third Friday of each month during the school year, and every Friday in July and August (9 AM). Reservations are required; free. The fed has plans to create a New England Economic History Museum; call for current information.

Quiz time: what is the third largest financial center in the world, after New York and London? Number two: what is the mutual fund capital of the world (hint: mutual funds were originally called Boston Funds)? Three: what's the second largest center in the world for investment management? Answers: Boston, Boston, Boston.

How'd you score? If you got all three questions wrong, it's time for a trip to the **Boston Stock Exchange** (100 Franklin Street, entrance at 201 Devonshire Street, 617-235-2223), where exhibits and interactive screens will fill you in on all that glitters, albeit virtually, in Beantown. Few people are aware that, high above the BSE's trading floor, there is a fascinating visual display telling the story of commerce in the Bay State, from codfish and wampum beads to Polartec fleece, Converse All-Stars, and Lotus spreadsheets. If you can tear yourself away from the beaver pelts and boxes of Fig Newtons, a glance at the 21st century awaits; from the glass windows of the mezzanine, you can gaze down on the BSE trading floor, where 15 million shares change hands on any given day. Unlike the New York Stock Exchange, there's no voice trading here (it's all computerized), so what you're watching is a bunch of men (and one or two women) hunched over computer screens sipping black coffee. As you might imagine, this loses its charm fast, but a bank of interactive computer screens saves the day, providing answers to all your fiduciary questions, except how to save your dotcom. Remember your visit with a T-shirt or golf balls emblazoned with the BSE emblem. Be sure to call the Boston Stock Exchange in advance of your visit, as the public area was closed for reasons of security — either temporarily or permanently — at time of publication.

SECRET

MOUNTAINEERING

Among the many nonprofit headquarters on Beacon Hill's Joy Street is the venerable **Appalachian Mountain Club** (3 Joy Street, 617-523-0636). You might easily miss it — garish displays are *verboten* here on

Joy — but inside this typical Beacon Hill townhouse is a comprehensive selection of outdoor exploration books and guides with titles ranging from Rachel Carson's *Silent Spring* to Bill McKibben's *The End of Nature.* There are maps, too, as well as a few hiker gadgets. Even if you're not heading for the hills, an AMC compass might help you to get around the twisted streets of Boston. Members get a discount, but anyone can shop here. Open weekdays (8:30 AM to 5 PM). The public is invited to enjoy the regular slide and lecture presentations that take place here of an evening, when mountain climbers, photographers, and wildlife experts regale the crowd with tales of adventure and sore feet. Call, or check the bulletin board in the entryway for times.

You don't have to head for the Appalachian Range for a trek. The Blue **Hills Reservation** (visitors' center, 695 Hillside Street, Milton, 617-698-1802) has 125 miles of hiking trails, not to mention horseback riding, fishing at **Houghton's Pond** (license required), rock climbing, and both cross-country and downhill skiing. To the north of the city, the **Middlesex Fells Reservation** (781-662-5230) has miles of trails (see "Secret Cycling" for maps). There are also nature trails throughout **Boston Harbor Islands National Recreation Area** (617-223-8666), where walkers connect the dots on free inter-island ferry rides.

S E C R E T
MOVIES

Every American city has its industriplex movie mall featuring butter-flavored popcorn and Hollywood-flavored films. But only Boston (the Cambridge part) has the Brattle. In addition to popcorn with real butter, the **Brattle Theatre** in Harvard Square (40 Brattle Street, Cambridge, 617-876-6837) has a brilliant menu of vintage and current celluloid every night of the week. Its theme nights change with the appearance of each much-anticipated calendar, from film noir to directors' retrospectives (Greenaway, Coppola, Fellini) to recent raves, Italian horror, or whatever else leaps from the fertile minds of the programmers. The theater has been renovated recently. The spring-loaded, 1970s-vintage seats were replaced, although I never heard anyone complain about them; they were part of Brattle aura. You can't fight progress.

The **Coolidge Corner Theatre** (290 Harvard Street, Coolidge Corner, 617-734-2500) does longer runs of independent, classic, and art films in its big Art Deco theater, while the balcony has been carved out as a smaller, but not miniscule, screen.

Film guru David Kleiler, former artistic director at the Coolidge, is now at the helm of **Local Sightings** (617-975-3361, www.localsightings.com), screening the works of New England filmmakers throughout Greater Boston. Check the Web site for a schedule. Two other forums for Boston and New England filmmakers are *Phoenix* film critic Gerald Peary's **Director's Cut** series, also at the Coolidge Corner, and the **Underground Film Revolution** (617-524-7677), a weekly indie film series in Jamaica Plain. For the complete story on local filmmaking, see New England Film's truly awesome online magazine and resources pages (www.newenglandfilm.com).

Very much worth keeping on your movie radar are the **Harvard Film Archive** (Carpenter Center for Visual Arts, 24 Quincy Street, 617-495-4700) and the **Museum of Fine Arts** (465 Huntington Avenue, 617-369-3907). Both have fine year-round film programs. Nothing is too obscure for these artsy venues, but don't be surprised to see slapstick and cartoon festivals as well. The **Nickelodeon** (606 Commonwealth Avenue, 617-424-1500) and the **Kendall Square Cinema** (1 Kendall Square, Cambridge, 617-494-9800) are both known for their high-brow and art-house programming. The 1925 **Wang Center** (268 Tremont Street, 617-482-9393) does a classic film series each year on its amazing 23-foot-tall screen, the largest in New England. The series features big films that lend themselves to the scale of this deluxe theater. Think *West Side Story, Lawrence of Arabia,* and the *Star Wars* trilogies.

In addition to these venues, there are scores of film events around the city. In summer, families haul lawn chairs, blankets, and industrial-sized bags of cheese doodles down to the Charles River Esplanade for the **Friday Flicks** (Metropolitan District Commission Hatch Shell, Charles River Esplanade, 617-727-1300, ext. 555, or 617-787-7174). From Memorial Day through the end of September, as dusk falls, a G- or PG-rated, full-length feature film jumps to life on the giant screen at the Hatch Shell. Also, many of the branch libraries show **children's films**. Check the *Boston Sunday Globe*'s "City Weekly" calendar section for listings. The **Boston Public Library** (700 Boylston Street, 617-536-5400) also has free classic film screenings on Monday nights.

Bostonians who'd rather stay home have a friend in local entrepreneur Marshall Smith. When Smith's former video store, purchased by a corporate chain a few eons back, went bust, Mr. Smith re-entered stage left, bought back the flagging Coolidge Corner branch, and resurrected it as **CinemaSmith** (283 Harvard Street, Brookline, 617-232-6637). A welcome addition to the art-rare-foreign-indie video scene, CinemaSmith is a big bright space staffed by a bunch of movie maniacs. The store boasts the largest and most diverse foreign film section in Boston, a growing gay and lesbian section, and smart thematic displays, from baseball movies to the American Film Institute's "100 Best Films of the 20th Century." There's a library of cinema reference books to help you find that out-there title. And while CinemaSmith has all the stuff fans of *cinema obscura* expect, it's also got scores of DVDs, multiple copies of the latest releases, and a supermarket-size selection — without the supermarket attitude.

Finally, if nothing will do but to be *in* a film or video, check the **Extras Hotline** (617-973-8800, www.state.ma.us/film/hotline.htm) operated by the Massachusetts Film Office. Or look up casting companies at New England Film's Web site (above).

S E C R E T
NORTH END

First home of the Puritan settlers, the North End has since welcomed succeeding waves of immigrants over the years: the Irish, then Russian and Polish Jews, then the Spanish and Portuguese, and finally the Italians, who came from the south of Italy after unification.

Today, many of the old high-rise tenements that housed these new-comers are high-end condos, but the North End remains a hub for all things Italian. Beyond Hanover Street — the only street in the neighborhood that's been widened to suit the needs of modern traffic — a warren of narrow lanes winds through the neighborhood. Old folks sit on folding chairs out on the sidewalk, chatting, passing the time of day, and keeping an eye on things. Caffe patrons watch soccer games and sip their espressos. Diners take their evening promenade. And everywhere you go, the aromas of baking bread and roasting garlic scent the air.

Don't look for a supermarket in the North End; it's all specialty shops, many of them run for generations by the same family. Overlooking the Big Dig, but scrappily resisting its ravages, **Joe Pace's & Son** (42 Cross Street, 617-227-9673) is the largest and oldest general grocery store in the neighborhood. There's a little of everything here: olive oil, breads, sausage, cheeses. And at the deli they cut fresh sandwiches that you can eat at the sidewalk tables — front-row seats on the Dig.

Another Big Dig survivor is **Maria's Pastry Shop** (46 Cross Street, 617-523-1196). Never mind the M&M cookies in the window; this is a real Italian *pasticceria*. Owner Maria Merola came to the United States 30 years ago, got a job at the pastry shop, eventually bought it and changed it to suit her Neapolitan tastes. That means not too heavy on the sugar, no preservatives, and just-out-of-the-oven freshness. Try the bitter chocolate toto, pretzel-like egg and pepper taralle, honey nougat torrone, elaborate marzipan "vegetables," ricotta cheese pies, macaroons, and, of course, some of Boston's best cannoli filled to order. Come by in the morning around 7:30 AM, when the "clam shells," or sfogliatelle, come out of the oven — flaky buns stuffed with ricotta, candied fruit, sugar, and cinnamon. As in all Italian pastry shops, on church holidays such as Easter, Christmas and St. Joseph's Day, a host of seasonal, saintly confections decorate the shelves. Pasticceria fans should also check out the **Modern Pastry** (257 Hanover Street, 617-523-3783), and **Boschetto** (158 Salem Street, 617-523-9350), where the breads are baked in a 120-year-old brick oven.

Where do these bakeries get their ingredients? **Dairy Fresh Candies** (57 Salem Street, 800-336-5536). Sharing shelf space with a rainbow of sugar sprinkles, coconut flakes, and chocolate bits are dried and candied fruits (flame raisins, cherries, cranberries, pears, and beautiful Saudi Arabian dates), sun-dried bell peppers, hard candies filled with grappa (murderously strong alcohol), real Italian licorice, and crystallized ginger from Australia and China. Nuts of the world — pignola (pine nuts) from China and Italy, dried chestnuts, and hazelnuts — are piled high on the counters, and there's also a Japanese snack: dried green peas covered in spicy wasabi horseradish sauce. On the opposite side of the tiny shop is a wall of condiments (jams, jellies, sauces) and the chocolates counter, as well as a selection of imported olive oils and real, aged balsamic vinegar. Here, too, the holidays bring seasonal goodies, from penny candy and pumpkin fudge in October to chocolate eggs at Easter.

At **Polcari's Coffee** (105 Salem Street, 617-227-0786), the air is scented with licorice, cinnamon, oregano, and oily coffee beans, roasted onsite. Everything is sold in bulk here, so shoppers can buy just as much as they need. There are vials filled with flavorings (anise, black currant) to add to coffee and liqueurs. Coffee beans are available roasted or unroasted, and you can also buy stovetop espresso makers. Along the outside wall are bins of beans, rice, and grains — staples of the Mediterranean diet — as well as exotic flours like chestnut and rye. If you're feeling hungry between meals, try a twig of real licorice root (35 cents a branch) or roasted and salted chickpeas for snacking.

Of the North End meat markets, **Salumeria Italiana** (151 Richmond Street, 617-523-8743) is the king. Sopressata, capicola, abruzzese, pancetta, mortadella and more are available for tasting. Also taste and buy the great cheeses of Italy here, from parmesan reggiano and stinky pecorino romano to mild table cheeses like asiago and pecorino ricotto salata. They also have rustic breads and *artisanal*

dried pasta (extruded through bronze rather than Teflon). It's twice the price of regular pasta, but well worth it as its rough surfaces "hold" the sauce better. There are premium canned Italian tomatoes, condiments including Italian tuna in glass jars, caperberries for your antipasto platter, a phenomenal selection of olive oils, and the best price in the neighborhood on dreamy balsamic vinegar. This place is firmly on the tourist trail and can get mobbed, but no matter: it always vibrates with Italian soul.

For your Italian veggies, stop by **Albe Produce** (18 Parmenter Street, no phone number available), where everything is purchased in small quantities and in season. Look for broccoli rabe, turnip greens, savoy cabbage with curly leaves and a sweeter taste than the grocery store variety, huge fans of escarole, bitter dandelion greens, bulbs of fennel, purple skinned garlic, tiny white eggplants, and fresh fava beans to eat raw out of the shell.

Owned by a third generation of Ciraces, **V. Cirace & Sons** (173 North Street, 617-227-3193, 800-843-7772) is not just a pretty face. Granted, the store is attractive and jazzy, but it also has a phenomenal selection of imports. For an *aperativo*, work your way through a dozen or so flavors of sambuca. Or try Limoncello from the Amalfi coast, redolent of lemons and sunshine. Sogno di Sorrento is a nice brand. For after-dinner drinks, there are *amaros* ("bitters"). Some 300 varieties of bitters are made in Italy; Cirace carries a selection of their favorite dozen or so. Italians swear by these digestives, which, as the name suggests, help diners digest their dinner — and better still, allow gluttons to move on happily to dessert. Also, check out the selection of sparkling wines at two for $20.

Until 15 or so years ago, most North End restaurants were cooking Italian-American food — meaty, cheesy dishes, heavy on the tomato sauce. Then came a wave of chef-entrepreneurs who started cooking authentic Italian *cucinare*. Now even the old guard is starting to change. There are scores of great restaurants in the North End. My current favorite is **Maurizio's** (364 Hanover Street, 617-367-1123), where the Sardinian fare is superb. The interior's warm red walls make dining here feel like swimming in the bottom of a bottle of Chianti. Try the linguini con calamari and expect perfect pasta sauce with just a little pepper bite, and fresh calamari, which you can enjoy with one of the lovely Sardinian house wines. If you can get a window seat, you'll watch pigeons flocking around St. Stephen's Church. For another Italian restaurant rave, try Gusto (see "Secret Rozzie Village").

There's so much to discover in the North End that it helps to have a knowledgeable guide. Michele Topor, who I can thank for much of my North End knowledge, is a whirling dervish of foodie wisdom. Topor takes visitors around her neighborhood on **North End Italian Market Tours** (617-523-6032), telling them about her favorite food shops, from the butcher to the baker to the greengrocer, fishmonger, and wine merchant. Along the way there are tastes of prosciutto (cured ham), biscotti (crisp, twice-baked cookies), fresh fava beans, roasted chickpeas, and liqueurs, as well as encounters with the neighbors ("Ey, Michele, whatchou doin'?"). You'll learn how to buy mozzarella di bufala (buffalo milk mozzarella), how to cook pasta, and how to drink cheap wine. If you only have a day to spend in the North End, take Topor's morning tour to allow the rest of the day for all the shopping and dining she'll inspire you to do.

S E C R E T
NOVELTIES

After years of visiting **Joie de Vivre** (1792 Massachusetts Avenue, Cambridge, 617-864-8188), ostensibly shopping for gifts, I finally had to admit my real reason for going there: to play. There's always a new gadget to fiddle with: a wonky puzzle, a way-out picture book, oddball jewelry, spinning tops, wind-up toys, scatological gags, and a library of art postcards. The owners encourage shoppers to try things out, so go ahead: play.

"Recklessly treading the fine line between novelties and natural history," **Flyrabbit** (155 Harvard Street, 617-782-1313) could be thought of as Joie de Vivre's evil twin. Allow me to set the scene: A young woman in white and black face paint, dog collar, and various chains, buckles, and accoutrements that clank each time she moves is negotiating a tattoo for the back of her neck. The tattooist warns that what she's asking for might take awhile. Not to worry: "Me and pain," she says, drawing two fingers together, "we get along." The backdrop for this charming drama is the most fascinating collection of objects this side of a museum. Like any smart retailer, Flyrabbit creates the need for its wares: antique lab specimens suspended in formaldehyde. Gotta have it. A skinned and headless rat, eerily beautiful in yellow and pink. Do the colors match your décor? Meanwhile, the book section offers titles on natural history, true crime, cults, and more. And, yes, they do tattoos. I think I need one of those, too, 'cause, me and pain . . . oh, never mind.

SECRET

OUTLETS

The **Dakini Factory Outlet** (574 Boston Avenue, Medford, 781-395-8113), in the heart of the Tufts University campus, has all the markings of the classic outlet: a cavernous space filled with seconds, slightly shop-worn goods, and out-of-season fashions at rock-bottom prices. There's rarely a crowd here, either. Known for its fleece blankets and oh-so-cozy pullovers, Dakini also designs floaty linen and cotton dresses, skirts, and tops. It has both men's and women's clothing, as well as a few children's items. Ask about the winter "blanket blow out" sales. Open Wednesday to Saturday (10 AM to 6 PM), and Sundays (noon to 5 PM).

Only open three days a week, **Frugal Fannie's Fashion Warehouse** (380 Western Avenue, Brighton, 617-783-3737) boasts acres of brand names, from Jones New York to Nine West to Versace. Grab a shopping cart and plow. The picking's always good, but the best thing about Fannie's is the vast changing room, where there is no limit to the number of items you can bring in. A social event in itself, the scene inside ranges from frenzied to friendly, with women dressing up and down, commenting, and occasionally helping neighbors with zippers. Open Fridays (10 AM to 9 PM), Saturdays (8 AM to 7 PM), and Sundays (11 AM to 6 PM).

SECRET

PARKING AND DRIVING

Nearly one million vehicles enter Boston each day, on the prowl for 100,000 parking spaces. That's 10 cars per spot. So, if you're hoping I have a secret parking space for you, "Dream on pal!" (as any native Bostonian might say).

Instead, I refer you to the crystalline prose of the 10th edition of *Car-Free in Boston*, available in most area bookstores. This little gem, published for 20 years by the Association for Public Transport, is the ultimate guide to getting into and around Boston (as well as eastern Massachusetts) cheaply and conveniently without your automobile.

There are, of course, parts of the city where a car is key. While I would not recommend taking a car into Downtown, Chinatown, the Financial District, the North End, or Beacon Hill (all easily accessible by T), there are places outside these neighborhoods where parking is available for those with luck and a handful of quarters. In the Back Bay and South End, parking is extremely tight, but around 6 PM — as office workers are leaving and before evening revelers begin to arrive for dinner and shows — a transition takes place and you might find a spot with relative ease. The same goes for Harvard Square, Cambridge. Outside these areas, the rest of Boston and Cambridge offer parking for some of the people some of the time.

Now, actually finding your way around Boston is an entirely different story. Walt Whitman said it best: "Crush up a sheet of letter-paper in your hand, throw it down, stamp it flat and that is a map of old

Boston." Actually, I'm not sure what he meant by that, but if Walt was trying to say that Boston's geography is a touch chaotic, he was right on the nose. And not much has changed since "old Boston" became new. Streets still twist and turn uncooperatively, many of them lack signs (the thinking being that if you don't know where you are, you shouldn't be there), and the Theater District has a mysterious intersection where Tremont Street meets Tremont Street. We also have the Big Dig. Slated to be completed by 2005, this gigantic public works project has turned the downtown area into a maze of Jersey barriers, glory holes, and Goldbergesque detours, causing even veteran Bostonians (yes, people do drive Downtown, go figure) to get hopelessly lost on occasion. On the bright side, as one Boston wag has said, "It's like, 'Everything was findable before the Big Dig!' Right." Until the dig is done and the dust clears, Bostonians and their visitors will continue to put up with I-93, rated as one of the top 10 worst city expressways in the country by the American Automobile Association. On the truly bright side, the Big Dig has become an attraction in itself (see "Secret Big Dig").

SECRET
PATRIOTS

Until all too recently, the only father and son to have been elected to the presidency of the United States were Bostonians John Adams and John Quincy Adams, the second and sixth presidents. With the election of the 41st and 43rd presidents, the Adamses are enjoying something of a boost in notoriety. Their rustic birth sites can be visited in Quincy — two side-by-side restored "salt box" houses of 17th-century vintage on their original foundations — along the old coast road from Boston to Plymouth. What makes the trip to Quincy worthwhile, however, is the Adamses' "Old House," built in 1731. Purchased by John and Abigail in 1787 and the home of four generations of Adamses, the house is exquisitely preserved, from the chair where old John died to John Quincy Adams's "presidential" library of 14,000 books. A beautiful formal garden surrounds the house. Trolleys from the **Adams National Historical Park** visitors' center (135 Adams Street, at Newport Avenue, in a mall across from Quincy Center T station, Quincy, 617-770-1175) take visitors to the Adams sites between mid-April and mid-November. The visitors' center opens at 9 AM daily, and the first trolley departs at 9:15 AM and every half hour through the day for the two-hour tour; $2.

You say you want a revolution? Book the **Old South Meeting House** (310 Washington Street, 617-482-6439). Some of the American Revolution's fieriest speeches took place here. In those days, it was the largest meeting hall in town (bigger, for example, than Faneuil Hall; see below). When the building was to be demolished in 1876, a bevy of prominent Bostonians — including Julia Ward Howe, Ralph Waldo Emerson, and Wendell Phillips — rallied to save the building. Today, the exhibition "Voices of Protest" traces the Old South's historical role in Boston's free speech movement and the hall's 300-year history as a gathering place for religious, political, and social debate, ever since the night in 1773 when Samuel Adams launched the Boston Tea Party here. The tradition continues with "Middays at the Meeting House" lectures (as well as concerts).

Pronounced "*fan*-yuhl" or "*fan*-uhl" — take your pick — **Faneuil Hall** (Boston National Historical Park, 617-242-5642) remains true to its original purpose as a marketplace, though postcards and T-shirts have replaced fish and produce. But quietly biding its time above the first-floor souvenir shops is the Federal meeting hall, where National Park Service rangers hold forth on what went down here during the 18th century, when Samuel Adams and his "Sons of Liberty" denounced British rule. Over the years, the walls of this room have vibrated to other orators: William Lloyd Garrison as he appealed for an end to slavery, Susan B. Anthony on the second-class status of women, and John F. Kennedy giving his last pre-election speech in 1960. The hall can still be rented out for meetings, political and otherwise, but it's strictly against the law now to plot to overthrow the government here. Times change.

On the third floor of Faneuil Hall is the obscure little museum and armory of the **Ancient and Honorable Artillery Company of Massachusetts** (617-227-1638). Founded in 1638, the company has occupied a space in Faneuil Hall since the 18th century. Open weekdays (9 AM to 3:30 PM); free.

One of the biggest flag-waving events on Boston's calendar is the Boston Pops' annual **July 4th Esplanade Concert**. Expect some 500,000 or so spectators to sing along with the Pops on patriotic numbers from "America the Beautiful" to "Yankee Doodle," while spectacular fireworks burst forth from river barges. If you don't care to share your picnic with half a million others, arrive a day early (July 3) for the **dress rehearsal** and enjoy the Pops, tuxedoes and all (but no fireworks). If you must have the works, try watching the event from the giant screen at the Top of the Hub (Prudential Center, Boylston Street, 617-536-1775) or live out the windows of Zephyr (Hyatt Regency, 575 Memorial Drive, Cambridge, 617-492-1234). Of course, you may get some stares if you sing along there. There certainly will be no singing along, anywhere, to the concert-fireworks finale, Tchaikovsky's *1812 Overture,* played to the accompaniment of National Guard cannons.

A lesser-known July 4th event is the annual morning **reading of the Declaration of Independence** from the balcony of the Old State House. It's part of the giant Harborfest kerfuffle, when some 2.5 million people converge on the waterfront for seven days of historical reenactments, walking tours, concerts, harbor cruises, chowder slurping, and fireworks. At any time of year, bring two hankies to the **Old State House Museum** (State and Washington streets, 617-720-1713) for the seven-minute documentary on the birth of our nation. Then troop up the central spiral staircase to the exhibition hall, where there is a display on Boston's major fires, including the 1942 Cocoanut Grove conflagration on Piedmont Street when 400 people died, mostly of smoke inhalation. (Aside: firebugs will appreciate, as well, the **Boston Fire Museum**, 344 Congress Street, at Farnsworth Street, 617-482-1344; open Saturdays, noon to 4 PM; free). Also profiled at the Old State House is the Boston Massacre, which took place just out front. Bringing these and other historical events to life are recorded speeches and letters read by actors, such as Abigail Adams's account of the wild scene around the State House at the first reading of the Declaration: "Thus ends royal authority in this state and all the people say 'Amen.'" Open daily (9 AM to 5 PM); $3. By the way, it was author and physician Oliver Wendell Holmes who called the Old State House "the hub of the Solar System." Time altered the statement to "Boston is the hub of the Universe," and finally just "Boston: The Hub."

John Singleton Copley's pre-Revolutionary **portraits** of Hancock, Revere, and Samuel Adams hang at the **Museum of Fine Arts** (465 Huntington Avenue, 617-267-9300) as do — sometimes — Gilbert Stuart's even more famous unfinished paintings of George and Martha Washington. In 1980, the MFA and the Smithsonian Institution purchased George and Martha from the Boston Athenaeum (see

"Secret Art") for $4.9 million. The Athenaeum let the First Couple go with the stipulation that the museums share the paintings: three years in Boston followed by three years in Washington, and so on.

Created in 1951, Boston's **Freedom Trail** (www.the-freedomtrail.org) — a red "line of liberty" painted on the sidewalk linking 16 notable American Revolutionary sites — is an extraordinarily beaten path. Thousands of tourists toe the red line each year. The **National Park Service** (15 State Street, 617-242-5642) offers guided walks of the 2.5-mile trail, which snakes from the Boston Common visitors' center through downtown and the North End, and into Charlestown.

S E C R E T
PATRON SAINT
✤

The patron saint of Boston isn't Patrick. It's Botolph, Anglo-Saxon for "the Boat Helper" (bot holph, get it?). St. Botolph is the borrowed martyr who came along with a borrowed town name, Botolphs Town, original English home of many of the Puritan exiles. It was later rendered Bottleston, then Bottston, and finally, in a fit of garbled enunciation brought on by one too many English ales, Boston.

But hang on. Before our own fair city was dubbed Boston, it was called "Trimountain" in honor of the three steep hills that towered over the Shawmut peninsula. Of the three hills, only a much scrawnier Beacon Hill remains today. The others were obliterated and used as landfill. In 1630, the settlers voted that "Trimountain be called Boston." Tremont Street is derived from Boston's original moniker.

SECRET

PENNY CANDY

Past the candy-striped awning, past the window full of colored pencils, erasers, gum, and jigsaw puzzles, Ethel sits comfortably in a folding aluminum chair inside **Irving's Toy & Card Shop** (371 Harvard Street, Brookline, 617-566-9327). She wears a handmade badge that reads, "I ♥ my customers." Surrounding her in the tiny Brookline shop are stacks of board games and school supplies, and piles of penny candy. An eight-year-old girl walks in clutching a dollar bill. "Well, hello," says Ethel. "You're Nicole, aren't you?" "Zoë," she replies. "Are you here visiting your grandmother?" asks Ethel. "Just remember," replies Zoë, arms akimbo, "when I'm here, I'm always visiting my grandmother. What are these?" she asks, pointing to some red pops. "Those are new," says Ethel. "They're sour on the inside and sweet on the outside." Zoë takes one and Ethel raises her eyebrows. "Do you need that?" asks Ethel. "I don't think so," she adds. Zoë starts counting out "warheads." "Twenty-five, 50 cents, 75 cents, a dollar," counts Ethel. "There," says Zoë, handing over the wrinkled dollar. "Okay, put those in your pocket," admonishes Ethel. "You'll drop them. See you next time."

SECRET

PICNICS

It's important to exercise your rights, one of which is to picnic on **Boston Common**. If you find yourself in "the country's oldest public space" sans victuals, head for Charles Street, where the first little grocery store you'll encounter is **Deluca's** (11 Charles Street, 617-523-4343), with its packed aisles of exotic imports intermingled with Kellogg's Corn Flakes and Joy dishwashing liquid. If you don't mind going a few more blocks, you'll find the truly gourmet **Savenor's** (160 Charles Street, 617-723-MEAT). This small space is packed with drool-inducing delicacies. In the bread department, look for *Iggy's* ficelle loaves, olive rolls, and thick focaccia (see "Secret Bakeries" for more on Iggy's). The cheeses come pre-sliced, or you can ask for a custom slice from the cheese cutter who also, a sign by the dairy case notes, happens to be a topiary artist. Look, especially, for goat cheese inlaid with pansies.

A hidden picnicking spot in the Leather District is the stone-paved courtyard of high-rise **Lincoln Plaza** (enter on Lincoln Street). Order a hot dish "to go" from a nearby South station vendor, or grab a sandwich and cold drink from the charming **Sagarino's** (106 South Street, 617-357-8855), and head for this oasis of flowering trees and sunshine. If you've forgotten something, you might find it at the tiny convenience store in the lobby. A word to the wise: this courtyard is not actually a public space, but if you're discreet and dressed in "business casual," you'll fit right in. Don't tell them I sent you.

A similar hideaway, but for a cold winter's day, is the aptly and yet not at all aptly named **Winter Garden** (222 Berkeley Street). Winter, yes. Garden, not really. Set in the glass-roofed courtyard of the Houghton Mifflin building, this vast marble-clad atrium with its drizzling post-modern fountains has very little greenery, aside from a couple of potted palms. But if you need a place to eat your tuna on rye in the Back Bay, you could do a lot worse than pull up a chair at one of several café tables here. FYI, you're at the back door of FAO Schwartz, and there's a tiny **Rebecca**'s outpost on the atrium serving hot drinks only. Open weekdays.

In Jamaica Plain, **Forest Hills Cemetery** (95 Forest Hills Avenue, Jamaica Plain, 617-524-0128) was Kahlil Gibran's (1883–1931) favorite picnic spot. The Lebanese-American essayist, poet, and painter is best known as the author of *The Prophet* and posthumous guest of honor at countless hippie wedding ceremonies. (There's a monument to him on Copley Plaza.) Unlike its sister cemetery, Mt. Auburn, Forest Hills allows noshing — not amidst the dearly departed, but by Lake Hibiscus.

Pick up a moveable feast at **Marché Mövenpick** (Prudential Center, 800 Boylston Street, or enter on Belvidere Street, 617-578-9700) — anything from sandwiches to pasta to seafood — for a banquet by the Christian Science Plaza, located directly across from the Belvidere Street entrance to the restaurant-market.

One day each year, picnickers have a fling at the **Arnold Arboretum** (125 Arborway, 617-524-1717), otherwise off limits to anyone wielding a potato salad. The banner day takes place on **Lilac Sunday**, the second Sunday in May, also known as Mother's Day. To add to the fun, Morris dancers kick up their heels around the park, lilac plants are for sale, and the arboretum's prize lilac collection — the star attraction — is at its seasonal height.

Across the river, **Cardullo's** (6 Brattle Street, Cambridge, 617-491-8888) was described in a 1965 article in the *Boston Traveler* as a "posh pantry . . . an edible encyclopedia." A quarter century later, Cardullo's remains as posh and edible as ever. It is *the* place to stock a **Cambridge Common** or **Charles riverbank** picnic with everything you need — right down to the hamper, hold the ants. There are gourmet foods, cheese, wine, chocolate. At the sandwich counter, ask for whatever you like: Perhaps a little pâté and slices of sweet pickles on a chewy baguette? You got it. Given its location, it may come as no surprise that you pay top dollar here.

These ideas for urban picnics are really just the tip of the iceberg lettuce. I urge you to strike out on your own. Like all arts, city picnicking is best learned by doing.

SECRET
PICTURES

I don't know about you, but I have my favorite paintings, and no amount of blockbuster show propaganda can dissuade me from visiting them from time to time.

If you visit the **Museum of Fine Arts** (465 Huntington Avenue, 617-267-9300), you'll no doubt find your way to whatever appeals to your own sensibilities, be they honed to Indian erotica, Egyptian mummies, or colonial portraiture. In any case, don't miss my favorite, John Singleton Copley's *Watson and the Shark,* made in 1778. In dramatic strokes, the painting tells the true story of the boy Brook Watson, who was nearly eaten by a shark. Copley's masterpiece oozes drama: the pale skin of the naked youth half submerged in the sickly green sea, the gaping red maw of the shark, the desperate rescuers. It's the *Jaws* of the 18th century. Open every day (from 10 AM; call for closing times as they vary by day); $15. On Wednesdays, the MFA offers admission for a suggested donation of $5 (4 PM to 9:45 PM). You should feel free to give what you can. It's best to go early before the crowds get thick, although during the summer, the Wednesday evening tumult has its perks, when musicians, sidewalk muralists, and children's activities pop up in unexpected corners of the museum and grounds.

One could argue that the most compelling reason to visit Boston lies in a single painting: Titian's *The Rape of Europa*. It hangs at the **Isabella Stewart Gardner Museum** (2 Palace Road, 617-566-1401), where Mrs. Gardner not only placed it but also built an entire Italianate villa around it. As well as the Titian (originally commissioned by Phillip II of Spain), Mrs. Gardner's collection includes Old Masters and Italian Renaissance paintings, works by Matisse and Whistler, and the city's only Michelangelo. But this is no ordinary museum. It was Gardner's home until her death in 1924, and it remains as she designed it; you get the idea that she loved these objects, not because she was supposed to, but because she just did. To see art here is to see it in the context of a life, rather than in the limbo of a typical museum gallery. Beyond the fabulous art, there is Mrs. Gardner's house to explore and appreciate. The rooms of the villa surround a four-story glass-roofed courtyard with Moorish-style windows and balconies. The courtyard is lushly planted with flowering shrubs and trees framing a second-century Roman floor mosaic.

The Gardner has a sweet little café and world-class chamber concerts on Sundays (1:30 PM). Open Tuesday to Sunday (11 AM to 5 PM); $10 on weekdays, $11 on weekends.

SECRET
PIZZA

In a cavernous hall decorated with Italian travel posters, a noisy North End lunch crowd waits patiently in line for juicy squares of cheese pizza and red wine in a Dixie cup. It can only be **Umberto**

Galleria (289 Hanover Street, 617-227-5709), a pizza joint that serves its 85-cent slices each day until they run out. Also on the menu are panzanoti, mashed potatoes wrapped around a nugget of mozzarella deep fried in bread crumbs, and a similar number with ground beef, as well as the most expensive thing on the menu, calzones with ricotta or spinach ($2.50).

Also in the North End, despite having opened a couple of franchises (at Faneuil Hall and the Burlington Mall), the original **Pizzeria Regina** (11 1/2 Thacher Street, 617-227-0765) hasn't forgotten how to make great pizza. Visit the mother ship for thin-crust pizza, topped with traditional ingredients, and a cold bottle of Coke. And if your waitress isn't ill-humored, it's not Regina's.

Over in East Boston, another Italian stronghold, **Santarpio's** (111 Chelsea Street, 617-567-9871) is thought by many to make the best pizza in Boston. While the atmosphere is that of a neighborhood sports bar, the pizza is world class: a thin, crisp crust topped with a mouth-watering sauce, followed by just enough mozzarella. Toppings are standard: canned mushrooms, onions, pepperoni, anchovies. My advice is to go for the plain cheese with a lamb kebab on the side. Did I mention they're cheap? Pies come in one-size-fits-all sizes, starting at $7.50 for a plain cheese.

SECRET
POETRY

Boston is a city of words. On most nights of the week, a poetry jam (open mic) or slam (competition) is happening somewhere. On

Sundays, the **Lizard Lounge** (1667 Massachusetts Avenue, Cambridge, 617-547-0759) hosts poetry slams and jams backed by the Jeff Robinson Trio; and the **Harvard Coop Poetry Exchange** (1400 Massachusetts Avenue, 617-236-7460) provides a mic for other aspiring bards. Mondays, **Stone Soup Poets** meet at the **Middle East** (472 Massachusetts Avenue, Cambridge, 617-227-0845) with featured writers. The **Agape Poets** share their latest works every Tuesday at the Community Church of Greater Boston (565 Boylston Street, 617-266-6710). On Wednesdays, the **Cantab Lounge** (738 Massachusetts Avenue, Cambridge, 617-354-2685) hosts a two-hour free-for-all open mic, followed by a featured poet and slam. The first Thursday of the month finds poetry aficionados at **Rhythm & Muse** (403A Centre Street, Jamaica Plain, 617-524-6622), where a headlining poet is followed by an open mic session. Fridays, poets stay home, presumably to try out their latest sestina in the shower. Rested and ready, wordsmiths return to the scene with **Out of the Blue Poetry Night** (Out of the Blue Gallery, 168 Brookline Street, Cambridge, 617-354-5287) every Saturday, with poetry and prose. Music is added to the mix every fourth Saturday of the month.

For additional spoken-word events, check out the listings each Thursday in the *Boston Globe* "Calendar" section, or pick up a free copy of the *Improper Bostonian* or the *Phoenix.*

S E C R E T
R & B

Cambridge's still-funky Central Square is R&B central. For nearly a quarter century, "Little" Joe Cook — a diminutive one-man musical hurricane of 78 years, clad in a blue leisure suit and gold necklaces — has gyrated nightly to his hit tune, "Sexy lady from the beauty shop! You make my heart go bippety bop!" downstairs at the seething, smoky **Cantab Lounge** (738 Massachusetts Avenue, Cambridge, 617-354-2685). Backed by his group, the Thrillers, Joe starts the night with "Come on you hamburgers and cheeseburgers," and the dancing begins. Not far from the Cantab, the **People's Club** (288A Green Street, Cambridge, 617-547-9320), a subterranean Veterans of Foreign Wars hall, promises "inexpensive drinks and a trippy light show," along with its lineup of local jazz, funk, and R&B heroes. For take-home R&B, visit Central Square's **Skippy White's** (538 Massachusetts Avenue, Cambridge, 617-491-3345), which stocks soul, rap, reggae, blues, gospel, Latin, and jazz as well. There's a second location in Jamaica Plain (315 Centre Street, Jamaica Plain, 617-524-4500).

Other places around town to see live R&B include **Harper's Ferry** (156 Brighton Avenue, 617-254-9743), the **Tam** (1648 Beacon Street, Brookline, 617-277-0982), and the **Western Front** (343 Western Avenue, Cambridge, 617-492-7772).

SECRET
RECYCLING

At twenty-something, I didn't have a stick of furniture. And, as a Harvard University office drudge, I didn't have a penny to spend on it. Not a problem. Then, as now, **garbage day in Cambridge** was a scavenger's paradise. Before long, I knew when all the best neighborhoods set out the trash, and my bare rooms began to take on a certain dumpy, post-modern *je ne sais quoi.* Since I now enjoy the extravagant salary of a freelance writer, I can afford to buy my furniture at yard sales (I don't mean to boast). But students and other down-and-outs continue the noble tradition and public service of salvaging the cast-offs of prosperous Cantabridgians.

Lately, recycling has become a fashion statement. Capitalizing on this trend, Gail Bohan created **Eco Interiors** (694 Broadway, Ball Square, Somerville, 617-623-0907), a gallery-showroom for furniture and housewares made from non-virgin materials. While the big-ticket items — beds and armoires made from the wood of old barns and used shipping pallets — are more showy than practical, the smaller pieces are fun. Recycling artisans transform mundane materials into utilitarian art, like an Adirondack chair made from skis, CD shelves built of bicycle parts, and stemware fashioned from recycled glass.

SECRET
REPRODUCTIONS

Occupying a barn-like building at Arlington's Old Schwamb Mill (see "Secret Industrial History"), **Shaker Workshops** (18 Mill Lane, Arlington, 781-648-8809) is the showroom of a Massachusetts enterprise devoted to making faithful reproductions of Shaker furniture and accessories, including wooden bowls, quilts, baskets, and round boxes. Modeling its designs after original Shaker furniture now in museums and private collections, the workshop stays as true as possible to both the design and the construction methods of the Shakers, though it does make modern adaptations, such as coffee tables and computer desks. The chairs, made from maple or cherry, are especially attractive — delicate and graceful, but surprisingly sturdy, ladderbacks with rounded finials and seats of woven fabric tape. You can buy many of the products here as kits for about half the price of a finished piece. Kits, which contain all the materials you need, are an excellent way to learn about the Shakers' ingenious methods of fabrication — and, in true Shaker fashion, save a bundle. Open Monday to Saturday (10 AM to 6 PM).

In addition to its mission of preserving old houses and their contents, the **Society for the Preservation of New England Antiquities** (SPNEA, 141 Cambridge Street, 617-227-3956) also partners with New England craftspeople who churn out finely crafted copies of textiles and furniture — many of them copies of pieces that the Society owns. The SPNEA publishes a catalog brimming with wallpapers, door knockers, drawer pulls, cabinets, chairs, and jewelry.

S E C R E T
ROCK
❧

Over the years, Boston's rock music scene has launched the careers of Aerosmith, the Cars, Jonathan Richman, Boston, and the Pixies, to name but a few. While the current state of the industry makes it more difficult than ever for a band to propel itself into the national spotlight, that doesn't stop scores of talented local bands from trying.

There are various proving grounds for Boston and New England bands, as well as for visiting acts, including the following. The **Middle East** (472–480 Massachusetts Avenue, Cambridge, 617-864-EAST) is the hub of the local rock scene. Nearby in Central Square, a young crowd packs TT **the Bear's** (10 Brookline Street, Cambridge, 492-BEAR) for alternative rock. National acts play here regularly, but Sundays, Tuesdays, and most Wednesdays are devoted to local talent. Club Bohemia at the **Kirkland Café** (427 Washington Street, Somerville, 617-491-9640) is a small, friendly place for aging punks. The tiny **Kendall Café** (233 Cardinal Medeiros Avenue, Cambridge, 617-661-0993) is a favorite of Boston rockers for its living-room-like atmosphere. Another way-small club, **Toad** (1912 Massachusetts Avenue, Cambridge, 617-497-4950), features acoustic rock. Uniquely, **Jacques** (79 Broadway, 617-426-8902) puts on garage rock in the downstairs bar, while drag queens put on outrageous frocks in the upstairs revue.

For the latest rock news, look for *The Noise* (www.thenoise-boston.com), a 'zine that's been a constant in Boston rock for two decades. Now online as well, this rock gossip rag features concert reviews, record reviews, and raw pix of the Boston rock panorama, as well as what's happening around town in all the clubs. To hear local talent and live performances on the airwaves, turn to the college radio stations. There are regular live shows on WMFO 91.5 FM and WMBR 88.1 FM, among others. Or check out **Radioboston.com** (www.radioboston.com, request line 617-776-1717, ext. 210), with live club broadcasts from TT's, Club Passim, and the Kendall Café, as well as live "EJS" (electronic disc jockeys) playing "all local music, all the time." The *Boston Phoenix* **Band Guide** (available online at www.bostonphoenix.com/supplements/band_guide/index.html) appears each spring with listings of groups by genre, from "a cappella" to "tribute." Also check out **Dirty Water** (www.dirtywater.com), a virtual museum of Boston rock and roll.

Treading the thin line between rock and theater, **Boston Rock Opera** (www.rockopera.com) hijacks singers and instrumentalists

from bands all over Boston to appear in its over-the-top performances. The Web site also has a whole-lotta links to Boston bands.

S E C R E T
ROOTS
✿

The message of the new **Dreams of Freedom Center** (1 Milk
Street, at Washington Street, 617-338-6022 or 617-695-9990) is
straightforward: immigrants built Boston and continue to contribute
mightily to the city. Yet telling the disparate stories of entrepreneurs,
students, slaves, and refugees is no easy task. This downtown
museum mostly gets it right. While the multimedia show — complete with fog, wind, lightning, and even odors — is entertaining,
the exhibits are both entertaining and informative, inviting visitors
to explore the Boston immigrant experience on a variety of levels.
Everywhere you turn there are compelling stories, including an inter-
view with former governor and erstwhile presidential candidate
Michael Dukakis on growing up Greek-American. And, of course,
the gripping story of the Kennedy family is here as well. You'll also
learn about the latest groups of immigrants: Kosovars, Sudanese,
Chinese, and many more. Finally, visitors are invited to sit behind a
curtain and record their own or their families' stories of immigration.
Open daily (9:30 AM to 6 PM); $7.50.

Using the Dreams of Freedom Center as a starting point, the **Boston
Immigrant Heritage Trail** (Boston History Collaborative, 617-350-
0358, www.bostonfamilyhistory.com) is a self-guided tour, available
online, through city parks, side streets, churches, burying grounds,

and buildings that illustrate the story of Boston's immigrant populations.

SECRET

ROZZIE VILLAGE

Roslindale Village is blooming. In the last half-decade, funky boutiques and upscale restaurants have begun populating this once-down-hearted shopping district. The area has long had a nucleus of ethnic, mostly Greek, bakeries and specialty food shops. Now smart planning and civic pride are ensuring that the old guard benefits while Rozzie grows into its villagey name.

Part of the vanguard of the Roslindale renaissance, **Fornax Bread** (27 Corinth Street, Roslindale, 617-325-8852) set up shop in 1997. By now, residents aren't sure how they'd get along without "their" bakery. Long before you swing open Fornax's screen door, the scent of fresh-baked bread announces itself out on busy Corinth Street. Inside, the recently revamped space has tables and a marble counter for customers to sit awhile and sip their coffee, nibble, and chat. Since the renovation, the bakery has added soups, sandwiches, and quiche to the menu. Named after the goddess of the hearth, Fornax is a neighborhood hub where neighbors catch up on the local gossip and admire one another's children. The kids, by the way, swear by Fornax's cinnamon twists and scones. For grown-ups, there are gooey pecan twists and buttery cranberry bread. (These guys are no strangers to butter and sugar.) And, of course, the divine bread. Opens at 7 AM.

Another of the trailblazers is **Zia** (22 Birch Street, 617-327-1300), whose owner Lesia Stanchak opened the first of the boutiques that now grace Birch Street. This women's clothing and gift shop is one of my Boston favorites. It's a place where buying a dress or a suit or a sweater doesn't damage my self-esteem or my wallet — unlike those places where either nothing fits (it's me, right?) or the things that fit I can't afford. Lesia stocks the store with elegant, floaty dresses, suits that are classic without being stodgy, arty jackets, and playful sweaters.

A few doors down is **Joanne Rossman Design** (6 Birch Street, 617-323-4301). A self-taught accessory designer, Rossman has set up a European-style atelier here on Birch Street. Drop by and see her at work on her industrial sewing machine, materials ready at hand. She sells the raw materials of her trade — bolts of shimmering taffeta, beads, buttons, and spools of silk ribbon — as well as the finished products, including scarves, fabric handbags, and knickknacks.

Decorate yourself at Zia and Joanne Rossman, then see about your home at **Ampersand Designs** (16 Birch Street, 617-323-4487). There, owner Kristen Keefe offers a selection of furniture — dining tables, chairs, chests of drawers, side tables — along with home accessories from throw pillows to area rugs. It's the sort of place you might go to get inspiration for a corner of your house that needs a lift.

All dressed up and nowhere to go? **Gusto** (4174 Washington Street, 617-363-9225) was the first of a string of new restaurants to come to Rozzie Village, and it's already a classic. This stylish Italian *trattoria* does a superb job. The setting is pleasant, with the dining room split into two intimate spaces, and the wait staff makes sure everything goes smoothly. I recommend starting with the polenta stuffed with gruyere, toasted and drizzled with marinara sauce. Follow that, perhaps, with fluffy pillows of ravioli filled with four types of cheese. Desserts are splendid things: try panna cotta floating in a pool of caramelized pine nut sauce. Main courses range from $10.50 to $19.50. Open Tuesday to Saturday (5 PM to 10 PM).

On the theory that you can never have too many Italian restaurants, Roslindale has just welcomed **Delfino's** (754 South Street, 617-327-8359). This new restaurant looks promising, boasting a chef formerly of Upstairs at the Hasty Pudding. **Café Lola** (14 Birch Street, 617-469-0995) is set to open soon, serving eclectic American cuisine and weekend brunch, possibly accompanied by a jazz combo on weekend nights. The **Village Sushi Bar and Grill** is also in the works.

Solera (12 Corinth Street, Roslindale Village, 617-469-4005) is Rozzie's new boutique wine shop, where vividly painted walls are decorated in serpentine cast iron and lined with a small selection of bottles priced from $5 to $65. There are plenty of wine shops with wider selections, but Solera offers warm, personal service especially appreciated by those who are not high-flying connoisseurs. Wine tastings happen on Friday evenings.

Emack & Bolio's (2 Belgrade Avenue, 617-323-3323) is set in a spacious coffee shop right across from the Commuter Rail station. One of the hits here is the "monster mash" ice cream. Imagine dumping the entire contents of a trick-or-treat bag (M&MS, chocolate chips, Snickers, etc.) into a mound of vanilla ice cream, and you'll have an idea what it's all about. Grownups appreciate E&B's New York egg creams in four different flavors, though a New Yorker friend of mine says "chocolate egg creams are the only ones worth talking about."

The **Roslindale Fish Market** (39 Poplar Street, Roslindale, 617-327-9487) offers Greek specialties along with the daily catch. Look for crisp rusk bread from Crete, jars of grape leaves, and cans of okra, as well as Greek feta and crates of fresh greens. **Gooches Bakery** (4140 Washington Street, 617-325-3928) does exotic varieties of wheat-free Italian pasta and breads. Call first; this is mostly a wholesale place, with fleeting retail hours. **Bob's Pita Bakery** (748 South Street, 617-325-1585), also known as Droubi Brothers, bakes its own pitas in all shapes and sizes. You'll find Lebanese imports and fresh produce here, such as flats of fresh figs and cactus pears, bins of red lentils, and the best spinach feta pita bread on earth.

SECRET
SALVAGE

Its name is uttered in dulcet tones by anyone who's ever renovated a Boston house (or dreamed about it): the **Olde Bostonian** (66 Von Hillern Street, off Dorchester Avenue, one block west of Columbia Road, 617-282-9300). This storehouse of architectural doodads prides itself on its constantly rotating inventory of large, oddly useful things. A hundred or so wooden mantels are stacked like dominoes along one wall. Doors of every description are filed so neatly, you almost expect them to be arranged in A-Z fashion ("F" for French doors, "S" for saloon?). Elsewhere in the sawdusty showroom are claw-foot tubs, plaster molding, Corinthian columns, pedestal sinks, toilets, bidets, stained-glass windows, and dozens of drawers of furniture hardware, from glass doorknobs to brass window locks. If you're not renovating, get creative: enamel "COLD" and "HOT" faucet handles make cool paperweights. An oak door with glass windows can be set up on trestles as a trendy kitchen table. Or take home a claw-foot tub for a backyard lettuce bed. Open Monday to Saturday (8 AM to 5 PM).

On a smaller scale, a number of antiques shops carry house fixtures. One of the more memorable ones is located in Dorchester Lower Mills. At **Dark Horse Antiques**, **Collectibles & Oddities** (2297 Dorchester Avenue, 617-298-1031), owner Robert Ferrini has crammed a multitude of furniture and architectural salvage into a wedge-shaped storefront. Open Wednesday to Sunday (noon to 5 PM).

SECRET
SANDWICHES

Once upon a time, an upscale Harvard Square condo was touted by its real estate broker as being "two blocks from Darwin's." That's **Darwin's Ltd.** (148 Mt. Auburn Street, Cambridge, 617-354-5233), the sandwich shop where loyal patrons line up at lunch hour for unusual sandwich combinations named after Cambridge places and people. These are the best sandwiches in Boston, made with fresh ingredients, beautiful bread, and — the kicker — superb sauces. The "Mt. Auburn," for example, has layers of smoked turkey, slices of ripe avocado, red leaf lettuce, and a sauce that tastes of horseradish and tamari. Have it on a choice of eight different breads, from rosemary garlic to classic rye. There are hot dishes, too (lasagna, for example), and crisp salads. Toward the back of the store, patrons buy sandwiches by the slice, made on yard-long focaccia, stuffed with roasted vegetables or, perhaps, chicken Caesar. En route to the cash register, there are sandwich *cookies* filled with peanut butter or mint cream and dipped in dark chocolate. There's also a choice selection of cheeses, wine, imported beers, dairy items, and produce.

No one's advertising their proximity to the **New Chardon Café** (25 New Chardon Street, 617-523-7790), but this humble downtown eatery does the best BLT (bacon, lettuce, and tomato) in town. At lunchtime, hard hats and office workers alike throng the tiny shop, place orders fast and loudly, and, after a short wait, muscle their way back to the counter to retrieve the sandwich *du jour*: red and juicy tomatoes, cool and crisp iceberg lettuce, hot and chewy bacon, and mayo, slathered on crunchy toast. Those with a big hunger go for the Super BLT.

SECRET
SCENTS
⚜

The "hard to find fragrance specialists" at **Colonial Drug** (49 Brattle Street, Cambridge, 617-864-2222) aren't hard to find. They're right in Harvard Square. It's the fragrances that are hard to find — except here, at the hard-to-find fragrance specialists. In short, Colonial Drug carries perfumes you can't find elsewhere. Even if your *eau de quoi* isn't hard to find now, someday it might be. When that day comes, you can be sure that this place will have it. Open weekdays (8 AM to 7 PM) and Saturdays (8 AM to 6 PM).

SECRET

SEXUALITY SHOPS

At **Grand Opening!** (318 Harvard Street, Coolidge Corner Arcade, Brookline, 617-731-2626), a fresh-faced couple is doing a little shopping. He holds a vibrator up to the light and opines, ". . . yeah, but if you get at all enthusiastic, that's just not going to hold up." She smiles and nods, pointing to a sturdier model. Nearby, a couple of women are passing postcards back and forth: "Hah-my-gawd, check out this one!" With a Breck-girl smile, a saleswoman (the shop literature claims: "knowledgeable") approaches a meandering patron to ask if she can help her with anything. "Just looking" is the reply.

Just looking indeed. But that's one of the great things about this tasteful, hidden-away Brookline sex boutique. It's not only OK to be open to all the manifest guises of human sexuality, but it is also OK to start out being a little embarrassed by them. The take-home message here is "be yourself, have a little fun, and go ahead — why not?" Owner Kim Airs has built a loyal following on that warm-fuzzy foundation.

On the shelves, in addition to "adult toys and fantasy accoutrements," are massage oils and lubricants, safer sex products, postcards, magazines, and videos. The shop stocks around 1,000 book titles, from *Basic Flogging for Urbanites* to *Lady Chatterley's Lover,* and patrons can plop down in one of the boutique's comfy chairs to dip into a book or two. While Grand Opening is not a secret, per se (it's been cited as "Best of Boston" in the local media several times over), what many people don't realize is that GO is also an educational institution. Check out the full calendar of events and demos (yes, demos) hosted by visiting experts, as well as the formidable Ms. Airs. Recent offerings have delved into "Fantasy Role Playing" and "Creative Bondage." Students have learned how to "Talk Dirty," "Make Your Own Erotic Video," or "Take it Off!" Graduates of the last of these (for women only) can follow up with "Stripping II," when the grads go to a suburban strip joint to perform for real. Grand Opening is open Monday to Wednesday (10 AM to 7 PM), Thursday to Saturday (10 AM to 9 PM), and Sundays (noon to 6 PM).

Billing itself as a "boudoir of sin," **Hubba Hubba** (534 Massachusetts Avenue, Cambridge, 617-492-9082) is yet another woman-owned shop. But this one's got other ideas. Suzi Phelps, the owner of this long-running fetish, punk, and goth store, sells what she calls "underground fashion," stocking an array of leather and latex clothing and hardware, and boasting "the largest selection of corsets in the area!" Well, thank goodness. Open Monday to Thursday (noon to 8 PM), Fridays (noon to 9 PM), and Saturdays (noon to 7 PM).

SECRET

SHOES

✦

Mel is sizing up a customer. He follows her to the back of the store. "What are you? Size nine?" he asks her. "Ten," she replies. Mel, who can't be an inch over five feet, looks up at her and laughs. "Well, I was close . . . Take a look at this catalog," Mel continues. He opens to a page and says, "How about that? You like that?" and she says, "Yeah, actually, that's pretty much what I'm looking for." Says Mel, "They're coming in next week. I'll hold them for you. What's your name and number?" At **Mel's Capitol Shoes** (307 Harvard Street, Brookline,

617-734-1411), it's not just about the shoes, which, by the way, are a charmingly eclectic mix of flowered terry cloth mules, Birkenstocks, trendy platform sandals, rubber Wellingtons, flip flops, and garden clogs. It's about Mel. It's about your precious feet.

Far away from the world of Capitol Shoes, the shiny DSW **Shoe Warehouse** (385 Washington Street, 617-556-0052) is bereft of anything resembling Mel. No one will guess your shoe size here. You'll be lucky to find anyone around who's not simply poised to ring you up. However, if you dream of oceans of shoes — "over 1,000,000 pairs!" scream the ads — this may be your Shangri-La. From runners to strappy things to patent-leather boots, although there's nothing terribly avant-garde here, there are a whole lot of high-fashion brand names floating about under bright lights at around half their retail price. Open daily.

Frugal Fannie's (380 Western Avenue, Brighton, 617-783-3737) shoe department is similar to DSW's, if not quite as vast. For something edgy, try **Allston Beat** (348 Newbury Street, 617-421-9555), where you can choose between paisley Doc Martens and six-inch spike-heeled boots. The **Garment District** (200 Broadway, Cambridge, 617-876-5230) has recently expanded its shoe collection and now offers a fab array of patent-leather platform boots, sparkle-plenty sandals, and urban combat wear.

SECRET
SOCCER

Boston's Oneida Club was the first organized soccer club in the United States. A monument on **Boston Common** (near Charles and

Beacon streets) memorializes the team which, between 1862 and 1865, "played all comers," noting that the Oneida goal was never crossed. So much for competition.

One wonders what the old Oneida Club would make of the **Boston Breakers** (866-462-7325). Captained by Olympic champion Kristine Lilly, the Breakers are the city's newly minted professional women's soccer team. Home games are played at Boston University's Nickerson Field and are typically sold out — packed with rafts of screaming teenage girls. In other words: totally awesome. The region's major league men's soccer team — cool in its own right — is the **New England Revolution** (617-931-2000, 877-GET-REVS), playing at Foxboro Stadium (Route 1, Foxboro).

SECRET
SOUTH OF
THE BORDER

Walk slowly around Maverick Square in East Boston and listen. As you pass the little shops and business concerns, doors swing open from time to time and the sound of Cumbia music drifts out onto the square. Over the last decade or so, this Italian-American enclave has been settled by large numbers of Latinos from Central and South America: Salvadorans, Guatemalans, Nicaraguans, Hondurans, Brazilians, Mexicans, and Colombians. Even Eastie's old-guard Italian groceries are catering to the newer residents. The **Bennington Market** (32 Bennington Street, 617-567-7082), which is noted — at least in my mind — for its huge basil plants, also grows and sells medicinal herbs popular with the Hispanic population. In a reverse gesture, **La Sultana Bakery** (40 Maverick Square, 617-568-9999) provides Neapolitan cakes for its Italian neighbors. But it is a steady stream of Latinos — who linger awhile for the music, coffee, conversation, and Colombian arepas, or cornmeal bread — who largely patronize this Maverick Square fixture.

Just across from the Bennington Market, the minute **Karen Market** (41 Bennington Street, 617-569-7382) is pure Latin. You'll find all the canned and frozen goods you need to make a Latin feast here, as well as a small selection of fruits and vegetables. Don't overlook the homemade frozen treats by the checkout counter. On a scorching hot day, there's nothing's better than dropping 50 cents for a frozen banana dipped in chocolate.

A tiny place in deeply residential Arlington, **Olé Mexican Grill** (203 Broadway, Arlington, 781-643-2299) serves delicious Mexican sit-down dinners. Delivered in the casual atmosphere we've all come to expect from a cantina, this small restaurant's food and service are a step above. Decorated with twinkling chili pepper lights, the dining room is barely bigger than the kitchen, and on warm nights, diners spill out onto sidewalk tables. The tortilla chips arrive hot with a side of the house chilled and chunky salsa. For an appetizer, try tamales wrapped just right in saffron-colored banana leaves. The main course of grilled vegetable burrito with molé has a nice barbecue flavor and comes with succulent veggies. Olé doesn't have a liquor license, which is a good excuse to try the Jarritos, a lightly sweet Mexican soda that comes in tropical flavors like hibiscus, grapefruit, and tamarind. You may have a short wait for a table, but once you're seated, the service is fast and friendly. Families really like this spot.

S E C R E T
STARGAZING

Quasar, Pulsar, Red Giant. Boston nightclubs? Nope. They're just a few of the "billions and billions" of night phenomena to be seen during regular open houses at two Boston-area universities, where astrophysicists are studying and mapping the universe.

Every clear Wednesday night, the Department of Astronomy at the **Boston University College of Arts and Sciences** (725 Commonwealth Avenue, Room 522, 617-353-2630) holds its open night. The evening begins with a short introduction by the curator, after which visitors can take a look at celestial objects through the department's telescopes. Call the afternoon of the program for an update; free.

On the third Thursday of each month, the **Harvard-Smithsonian Center for Astrophysics** (Phillips Auditorium, 60 Garden Street, Cambridge, 617-495-7461) opens its doors to the public at 7:30 PM for its observatory night. The program features a lecture aimed at the amateur, along with a telescopic gander up on the roof when weather allows. With the enlightened idea that "everything we learned about science, we learned from the movies," the CfA also sponsors Sci-Fi Movie Night on the first Thursday of the month. In the past, viewers have thrilled to such sci-fi classics as the 1957 flick *The Incredible Shrinking Man* and the pre-Apollo *Destination Moon* from the 1950s. Both observatory nights and movie events are free and open to the public.

During spring, the **Boston Park Rangers** (617-635-7487) sponsor **stargazing evenings** at Peter's Hill in the Arnold Arboretum (125 Arborway, 617-524-1717). Rangers provide the telescope, point out constellations, and explain how to tell a star from a planet.

SECRET
STUMPS

Cambridge woodworker Mitch Ryerson hates to see a tree stump go to waste. So when a city shade tree has to come down, whether because of disease, age, or other natural causes, Ryerson goes to work. So far, he's converted seven elm and maple stumps into public, sculptural seats. Among them are a roomy red chair on **Oxford Street** and a high-backed lounger on **Clay Street**. There are two throne-like numbers on **Lee Street**. The most beloved is the "Pooh House" on **Hurlbut Street**, a tall, hollowed-out trunk topped by a shingled roof and weather vane, and a sign that reads "Mr. Sanders."

SECRET
SURGICAL THEATER

Before the discovery of anesthesia, surgery was a matter of speed. Like runners breaking the four-minute mile, Victorian surgeons attempted to attain their goal: the three-minute amputation. From the archives of the **Warren Anatomical Museum** (see "Secret Anatomy") comes a doctor's description of his own leg amputation: "[A] black whirlwind of emotion, the horror of great darkness, and the sense of desertion by God and man bordering close upon despair [. . .] swept through my mind and overwhelmed my heart." Such was the agony of this grisly operation that a patient might die of pain if the operation went on too long. And it wasn't all that much fun for the surgeons, either, who had to listen to the patient's screams.

So it came as a relief to doctors and patients alike when John Collins Warren performed the first successful public demonstration of the use of ether anesthesia. The scene was Massachusetts General Hospital at what is today known as the **Ether Dome** (Bulfinch Building, Massachusetts General Hospital, 617-726-2397). Atop Mass General's copper-domed Bulfinch Building, this surgical theater was purposely set apart from the rest of the hospital to shield other patients from the cries that emanated from it. But on October 16, 1846, all was quiet. A painting at the Dome brings the operation vividly to life, showing dentist William T.G. Morton looking on as Warren removes a tumor from the bloody jaw of a blessedly unconscious Gilbert Abbott. The Warren Anatomical Museum has a photograph of the event. It's a reenactment; during the actual event, the photographer passed out.

Today, the Ether Dome functions as a museum, with a small collection of photos, a 19th-century anatomical teaching skeleton, surgical instruments, and mummies — and, if you listen carefully, the echoes of agony. Open Monday to Friday (1 PM to 3 PM) or by appointment. It's closed occasionally for staff meetings, so call ahead.

SECRET
SWIMMING HOLES

You can't even go swimming in Boston without being reminded of some crazy mystic poet fellow. The site of Henry David Thoreau's experiment in simplicity, **Walden Pond**, is Boston's favorite swimming hole. On a hot summer day, you'd be hard pressed to imagine the Concordian scribbling away in his cabin by the pond, to which it often seems that the entire city has decamped.

Thoreau (pronounced "thorough," with the accent on the first syllable) lived at Walden from 1845 to 1847, studying nature and coming to terms with the death of his brother. Yet, Thoreau's Walden was no more a wilderness than today's Walden. The train tracks along the western edge of the pond, now the MBTA Commuter Rail, were there already. ("The whistle of the locomotive penetrates my woods . . ." he wrote.) And while we usually picture the philosopher holed up in the deep dark woods, Thoreau brought his laundry home to mother and ate dinners at his family's nearby home. After Thoreau's day, things got really interesting around Walden. In the 1860s, an amusement park was built along the shores of the pond and most of the trees were cut down. It was only in the 1920s that the heirs of the Emersons, who owned the land, granted it to the state as a park. Since then, a second-growth hardwood forest has sprung up once again around the pond.

In keeping with its merry-go-round past, some 500,000 people continue to visit the 300-acre **Walden Pond State Reservation** (915 Walden Street, Route 126, Concord, 978-369-3254) annually. And, fittingly enough, most people come to Walden just to swim and sunbathe, walk the nature trails, or paddle a canoe — in short, to commune with nature. Recent improvements have done away with some of the rogue beaches that developed with use over the years, and the area around the pond has been preserved against further erosion.

For anyone interested in the history of the area, there is a museum and shop, a replica of Thoreau's cabin, and a historical marker at the site of the original cabin. The pile of stones beside the cabin site was started as a tribute to the departed writer by his friend Bronson Alcott, who visited in 1872.

Less crowded than Walden, and just as wet and cool, **Houghton's Pond** (Hillside Street, Milton) is located in the 6,000-acre Blue Hills Reservation. Situated around this glacially formed body of water are all the necessaries for a pleasant day of sunning and swimming, including free showers. There's an all-purpose snack bar, along with a pretty picnic gazebo overlooking the water, a playground, and a visitors' center with exhibits on the history of the reservation and pond. To boot, the Blue Hills have miles of trails. For a little adventure, park at the visitors' center (695 Hillside Street, Milton, 617-698-1802), pick up a trail map, and trek to the pond via one of the paths.

If you don't have time to head to a swimming hole, there are still plenty of places in the city center to chill. When temperatures rise in July, **Frog Pond** (Boston Common, near Beacon Street, 617-635-2120) becomes an enchanted prince of a wading pool, complete with spurting fountain and pool guards. Roll up your dungarees and splash a little. There's a snack bar offering edibles, and umbrella-shaded tables and park benches around the pond. Summer nights also bring jazz to Frog Pond (5 PM to 9 PM). Down in the North End, the **Mirabella Pool** (Commercial Street) looks out over the harbor. Right next to the scenic pool is a wading area, also with grand views of the USS *Constitution* and the Bunker Hill Monument. At the eastern end of the Christian Science Plaza, a corona of water jets spurts into the sky, making an irresistible water world for children and sizzling city workers. Even on moderate days, it's a lovely place to sit beneath the shade of a tree and enjoy a summer day.

SECRET

"T"

✽

The "T," short for MBTA, short for **Metropolitan Boston Transportation Authority**, is Boston's public transit system — a web of buses, trains, and electric streetcars that takes passengers around the Hub and out to the 'burbs. But Boston's T is as much a place to be as a thing that gets you there, forming a kind of linear venue for live music and public art.

Giving new meaning to the term "underground music," the **buskers** of Greater Boston's T stations run the musical gamut from classical to unclassifiable. Next time you pass one of these players, consider this: you may be listening to the next Tracy Chapman or Mary Lou Lord, both of whom got their start playing in Boston subway stations. Not content merely to sing there, artists have also written songs about the T, the most oft-sung being the Kingston Trio's tune about a stubborn guy named Charlie who refused to pay his return fare: "And did he ever return? No he never returned, and his fate is still unlearned. He may ride forever 'neath the streets of Boston. He's the man who never returned." Finally, **Club Passim** (47 Palmer Street, Cambridge, 617-492-7679) has been known to offer one-day crash courses on busking in Boston's subways and streets.

When T lines were extended in the 1970s and '80s, federal funding required that a certain percentage of costs be set aside for **art**. Exploring this underground gallery, you'll find photographs, murals, mosaics, kinetic sculpture, and ceramic tiles. At Porter station (Red Line), look for the lost and discarded gloves cast in bronze by Mags Harries for *The Glove Cycle*. Students from the Powder House

Community School in Somerville made the painted tiles at Davis under the supervision of artists Jack Gregory and Joan Wye. Some of the young artists (now in their 30s) commute to work daily past their permanent refrigerator art. At MIT/Cambridge Center, Paul Matisse's *Kendall Band* is a set of three aluminum and teak sound sculptures hung between the in-bound and out-bound platforms. T riders play them by pulling levers located on the platforms. The T (www.mbta. com) maintains a catalog of its entire art collection on its Web site.

S E C R E T

TEA

✢

Neither in Chinatown nor in the South End, but somewhere in between, the **Qingping Gallery Teahouse** (231 Shawmut Avenue, 617-482-9988) also hovers intriguingly between its mission as an art gallery and community gathering place and its role as a traditional Chinese teahouse. In the small, two-level teahouse, the curators mount shows of contemporary Chinese art, which, if the first exhib- its are any indication, will be among the finest and most quietly iconoclastic in the city. Chinese tea service ($3 to $7) begins with a few leaves dropped into a china bowl, steeped until just cool enough to drink. Built of rough wood, the interior of the gallery teahouse is a fusion of styles itself, with slate tabletops, bamboo lanterns, boul- ders with landscape patterns, and a collection of antique teapots. The background music, meanwhile, ranges from Chinese opera to jazz. Have your tea and almond cookie in the sunny front area, by the bubbling aquarium in the rear, or in the loft. Qingping also sells its wonderful teas by the gram and offers "tea education." Evening discussion groups on books, films, and "birds of the South End" are ongoing, and the gallery puts on frequent acoustic evenings.

At **Tea-Tray in the Sky** (1796 Massachusetts Avenue, Cambridge, 617-492-8327), the brew is served in glass samovars, kept warm at your table over a tiny flame. The tea is always lovely, but the popularity of this teahouse is also based on its creative, light food, as well as other hot drinks like the hot ginger and lemon infusion. The dessert menu is seasonal. For example, winter brings toasted bourbon pound cake with roasted fruit, caramel, and brown sugar crème fraîche. While waiting for a table, patrons browse through shelves of tea paraphernalia, from ceramic teapots and infusers of every persuasion to cozies, cups, and art inspired by the leaf. Look for the new, roomy, Arlington location (689 Massachusetts Avenue, Arlington, 781-643-7203), with a sunny tearoom out front and a full-service dining room in back.

Though a bit formulaic, I can't fault the **Tealuxe** (800-TEALUXE) chain for its 50-page tea menu; yes, as in five-oh. To accompany your brew, there are scones with Devonshire clotted cream and toasties. Check out the Golden Tippy Assam if you like a strong brew that can take lots of milk; one staffer described it to me as an "umphy" black. Tealuxe is spawning all over the Boston area. Look for branches in Boston at 108 Newbury Street, as well as in the Westin Hotel on Huntington Street; 256 Harvard Street in Brookline; Zero Brattle Street in Harvard Square, Cambridge; and 1223 Centre Street in Newton.

High tea is served Monday to Saturday (1 PM to 5 PM; $15) in the atrium of the **Inn at Harvard** (1201 Massachusetts Avenue, Cambridge, 617-491-2222, 800-458-5886). During the **Museum of Fine Arts'** (465 Huntington Avenue, 617-267-9300) annual Art in Bloom event, the MFA's **Ladies Committee** (yes, this is the 21st century and, yes, they're ladies) creates floral counterparts to selected artworks, and serves an elegant afternoon tea each day (2 PM to 5 PM; $10), along with piano accompaniment. Of late, the **Boston Harbor Hotel** (Rowes Wharf, 617-439-7000) has chimed in with a high tea of its own, daily (2:30 PM to 4 PM). You can also choose the unsavory-sounding yet patriotic "Harbor Tea" for about twice the price.

The **largest teakettle in America** gleams in gold leaf above what was for a long time a Scollay Square diner and is now, guess what, a Starbucks. Despite its current humiliation, the kettle has remained stationary, spewing its trail of steam while this part of Boston has transformed itself over and over again. It was created as an advertise-ment for the Oriental Tea Company and hung in 1873 making it, possibly, the oldest advertising sign in America. It's been steaming now for, let's see, 129 years. On one side is etched the kettle's capac-ity: 227 gallons, 2 quarts, 1 pint, and 1 gill (four ounces).

If you drink your giant tea English style with lots of milk, you'll be needing the giant milk bottle. Actually a vintage lunch stand from the 1930s, the 30-foot-tall **Hood Milk Bottle** (Museum Wharf, 300 Congress Street, no telephone number available) is today a Starbucks. Just kidding! The bottle remains the bottle and still serves sandwiches, snacks, and ice cream.

SECRET
TECHNOLOGY

"What is the meaning of life?" I typed into the computer keyboard. The answer came back, with typical cyber-alacrity, "Life is the character, state or condition of a living organism." Smarty-pants. This inter-active exploration of artificial intelligence is one of several perma-nent exhibits at the **MIT Museum** (265 Massachusetts Avenue, Cambridge, 617-253-4444). Sarcastic computers aside, what justifies the price of admission are Arthur Ganson's feats of "gestural engineer-ing," which fill several rooms of this university museum. Ganson's kinetic sculptures come to life when a curious onlooker touches a lever or presses a button: a tiny yellow chair explodes, then reassembles itself; a worm made out of metal mesh inches across a square foot of Astroturf. Also on permanent exhibit is Harold "Doc" Edgerton's pioneering work in strobe and underwater photography. Edgerton, who revolutionized photography when he created the electronic flash lamp in 1931, created scores of fascinating photos examining fast-moving objects like bullets, golf clubs, and milk drops. Another big attraction is the world's largest collection of holograms. That may sound way '70s, but this retro concept has been taken to the Nth degree here at MIT, where you can even watch a very short holo-graphic movie. Finally, there is the "Hall of Hacks," where campus pranks are immortalized — like the time a group of MIT students wrestled a cop car to the dome of the Alumni Center. Open Tuesday to Friday (10 AM to 5 PM), and weekends (noon to 5 PM); $5.

Also at MIT, the **Dibner Institute** (Burndy Library, 38 Memorial Drive, Cambridge, 617-253-8721) dedicates its rotating exhibits to the history of science and technology. A recent show featured gorgeous Japanese wood blocks illustrating the technological advances of the country through the 19th century. Browse through the visible storage anytime to see the brilliant collection of light bulbs. You heard me: ranged on tiered carousels, the antique bulbs show a range of subtle shapes, some with etchings, others with intricate filaments. Another prize part of the collection comprises, dare I say, "hair-raising" static electric generators. Open Monday to Friday (9 AM to 5 PM); free.

At Harvard, the **Collection of Historical Scientific Instruments** (The Science Center, 1 Oxford Street, 617-495-2627) is one of the world's largest collections of obsolete scientific equipment. Some 15,000 objects make up the collection, dating from around 1450 to the present, including Galileo's compass and a telescope owned by Benjamin Franklin. Open Tuesday to Friday (10 AM to 4 PM); free.

The **Museum of Science and Charles Hayden Planetarium** (Science Park, Monsignor O'Brien Highway, 617-723-2500) is a known quantity. I'll just note that having recently merged with the Computer Museum (formerly on Congress Street), the MoS is developing a new Current Science and Technology Center and already has some new digital exhibits. It looks promising.

S E C R E T
THEATER

Boston has the venues; its Theater District (according to the American Institute of Architects) boasts "the most outstanding group of early theaters in the country." It has the history; the old Shubert Theatre brought Sir Laurence Olivier to its stage, and the Wilbur Theatre premiered *A Streetcar Named Desire.*

So why doesn't Boston have a resplendent theater scene? First of all, it does. Second, you have to look for it.

You're not likely to find local theater gracing Theater District stages. New York imports and popular stars like Blue Man Group reign (as fun as they are, they're not Boston theater, no matter how you look at it). And, beyond thumbnail listings, you won't find much coverage of Boston's grudgingly underground theater scene in mainstream papers.

Instead, for intelligent reviews — heck, for any reviews — look to alternative papers like *Sojourner* and *Bay Windows*. Another resource is the comprehensive if quirky **Theater Mirror** (www.theatermirror. com). This online forum and soapbox for Larry Stark and friends is not exactly user-friendly, but it's one of the few places to keep abreast of what's going on in Boston theater. Lately, the Mayor's Office of Cultural Affairs has done theatergoers a favor by producing the smart quarterly, ***Boston Now*** (www.cityofboston.gov/calendar), which ferrets out cultural events that commercial publications often miss.

Of the more than 60 theater companies in Greater Boston — many with no permanent home — a lucky few companies find space each year at the South End's **Boston Center for the Arts** (539 Tremont Street, 617-426-5000). Around 20 small companies stage 45 works here each year, ranging from the avant-garde to classics to world premieres. With so many companies vying for Boston's limited performance space, the BCA plans to expand, adding a 40,000-square-foot facility that will include two performance spaces. Slated to open in 2003, these will be the first theaters to be built in Boston since the 1930s.

There's more good news in Cambridge, where the new **Market Theatre** (Winthrop Square, JFK Street, Cambridge, 617-576-0808) has taken up residence in a turn-of-the-century building. This 100-seat theater in the heart of Harvard Square showcases new works, as well as established works that rarely get a US viewing.

Boston's two leading theater companies, the **American Repertory Theater** (64 Brattle Street, Cambridge, 617-547-8300), associated with Harvard, and the **Huntington Theater Company** (264 Huntington Avenue, 617-266-0800), Boston University's resident company, both provide first-class drama. The ART leans toward cutting-edge interpretations and David Mamet premieres, while the Huntington takes a traditional approach to its wide-ranging, elaborately staged productions. August Wilson is a favorite and has premiered more than one of his plays here. Also in Harvard Square, radical student productions at the **Loeb Drama Center** (64 Brattle Street, Cambridge, 617-547-8300) are always excellent.

Summer brings al fresco theater out of the wings. One of the most promising companies is the **Commonwealth Shakespeare Company** (617-423-7600), which gives free performances at the Parkman Bandstand in Boston Common. The **Publick Theatre** (Christian Herter Park, Soldiers Field Road, 617-782-5425) does Shakespeare as well as Gilbert and Sullivan in its outdoor venue; $10 to $25.

Tastes aside, everyone loves a bargain. **BosTix** (617-262-8632) sells half-price tickets to selected shows at its booths in Copley Square and Faneuil Hall Marketplace. The booths are open daily (11 AM to 4 PM) for walk-up service only. BosTix doesn't sell Huntington tickets, but the company offers its own half-price ticket bonanza starting two hours before curtain, Tuesday to Thursday. The ART gives discounts to students only; call for details. Finally, if you must see Blue Man Group, at least have the decency not to pay for it. The **Charles Playhouse** (617-426-6912) offers free admission to volunteer ushers. Call to see whether they are "hiring." If so, all you have to do is wear black, arrive one hour before curtain, and stay 15 minutes after to help tidy up.

SECRET

THINGS THAT GO

Some people gripe that the T is so old and slow it's more like a museum piece than a modern transportation system. The grumblers have a point. While waiting for the clickety-clack of the next Green Line trolley at **Park Street station**, take note that you are in the oldest subway station in North America, inaugurated in 1897. One stop beyond Park, **Boylston station** is something of an informal museum. Hop off the trolley to take a look at one of the T's stock of vintage cars in an exhibit that changes periodically.

Another fine place to reflect on the history of getting there is the **Museum of Transportation** (15 Newton Street, Larz Anderson Park, Brookline, 617-522-6547). Set in the 19th-century carriage house of the Larz Anderson estate, this is the oldest collection of automobiles in the nation. The fabulously wealthy Anderson, along with his wife Isabel, began the collection in 1899, adding to it over the course of three decades. Today, the museum still features the couple's original collection of wheels, as well as a host of latter-day conveyances, including a couple of buffed-up 1970s muscle cars. Open Tuesday to Sunday (10 AM to 5 PM); $5. While you're there, be sure to take a stroll around Larz Anderson Park, with its lakeside promenade and lofty views of Boston.

Newbury Street promenaders might like to take a little detour in order to drool on the display windows at **Copley Motorcars** (441 Stuart Street, 617-421-9900). Along with a luxury or sport automobile *du jour*, the window displays a list of $50,000 cars up for grabs at this luxury car "boutique," from Range Rovers and Porsche Twin Turbos to Triumphs. In the same suite, **Vespa Boston** (441 Stuart Street,

617-425-6100) sells stylized Italian scooters and matching headgear in evocatively named colors like Grigio moonlight and dragon red. (As a little bonus, it's conveniently located next door to a spine and sports injury clinic.)

Should you find yourself in East Boston's Maverick Square (in search of the immaculate taco, perhaps), wander down Lewis Mall toward the waterfront along a fragrant meadow of Queen Anne's lace. On your left is the immense Port Authority's East Boston Pier No. 1, where the Teamsters Local 25 has its **driver-training program**. Watching a driver negotiate a tractor-trailer through a maze of orange cones gives one a sincere appreciation for what it takes to maneuver these big rigs. Eastie, for that matter, is a transportation freak's Mecca. Built over the Callahan Tunnel and under the nose of Logan Airport, and surrounded by water, the neighborhood provides scores of opportunities to watch the Hub go round and round. The best vantage is stunning **Piers Park** (95 Marginal Street), just the other side of East Boston Pier. Bring binoculars to the end of the promenade to see tankers and tugs, sailboats and kayaks bobbing in the harbor, or to spot jets arriving from all points of the globe.

S E C R E T

TIARAS

If I have any regrets, one would be that when asked, "Would you like to try on a tiara?" at **20th Century Ltd**. (73 Charles Street, 617-742-1031), I declined. I don't know what came over me. Still, it hardly mattered, and the charming owner of this Charles Street fixture didn't miss his chance to take me for a spin of his collection of jewel-encrusted diadems. Only a couple of the tiaras are antiques; the rest he commissions from artists in Boston and New York. There's even a tiny glittering headdress for Barbie and one for Jean Marshall, who, my guide explained, is "much more sophisticated" than her wasp-waisted competitor. The rest of this Charles Street shop is a cross between QE2's crown jewels and my grandmother's boudoir (my grandmother was very cool): dazzling cases of costume jewelry, pillbox hats decked with exotic flora. There's also silver flatware, prints, and assorted tchotchkes.

<h1 style="text-align:center">S E C R E T
TORY</h1>

While patriots and revolutionaries are trumpeted on the Freedom Trail, loyalists — those colonials who threw in their fates with King George — rarely get much attention. One of these forgotten Tories was William Shirley, a Royal governor of Massachusetts and commander-in-chief of British forces in North America. Hidden away in residential Roxbury, the **Shirley-Eustis House** (33 Shirley Street, 617-442-2275) was his country estate. Today, it is one of a very small handful of pre-Revolutionary buildings remaining in Boston.

The house was originally set on 33 acres overlooking the sparkling South Bay (now a shopping mall). Commander Shirley built his Roxbury estate on a much larger scale than most colonial houses at the time — a sign and symbol of British imperial strength. A popular governor, seen as being "one of us" (he was born in the US), Shirley died in 1771, just before all hell broke loose in the Colonies. During the Siege of Boston in 1775, the house was used as a barracks. Later, governor William Eustis owned the mansion, remodeling parts of it in Federal style.

As Roxbury's apple and pear orchards gave way to industry, Governor Shirley's old house was divided into apartments. It was saved from demolition by a group of citizens in the early part of the 20th century. The group found funds, restored the mansion during the 1980s, and opened it to the public in 1991. While it is largely unfurnished, that will change as renovations continue. Don't miss the map room, where etchings and paintings show how Boston's South Bay evolved over the last two or three centuries. Each year, the museum borrows a group of antique maps from the archives of the Boston Public Library for a thematic exhibition here. Tours are offered Thursday to Sunday from June to September (noon to 4 PM); $5.

S E C R E T
TOYS
❧

Two of the most basic instincts — putting things together and taking them apart — are exploited in equal measure at the **Construction Site** (200 Moody Street, Waltham, 781-899-7900), a toy store specializing in everything your budding engineer needs to create her or his world. "O"-laden brand names from Europe abound — Zolo, Brio, Lego — as well as stateside classics like Lincoln Logs. The youthful staff — as likely to be found toying with a fractal puzzle as dusting the merchandise — will help you locate what you're after, or leave you to play for hours with the Robotix computerized toys. Here, the trick is to get a tiny front-end loader to drive around a corner, pick up some blue boulders, and dump them in a railroad car. It's harder than it sounds. Also look for building block sets inspired by the designs of Frank Lloyd Wright and other famous architects. If you're heavily into realism, check out the Steinbauk line, where palm-sized wooden pallets are loaded with scaled-down terracotta bricks and roofing tiles. Add a miniature bag of mortar to your shopping basket and head home to model a tiny brick cottage or castle. Open daily.

Sometimes, you want to pretend you're crewing the Big Dig; other times, you just want to fritter away your allowance. **Animal**, **Vegetable**, **Mineral** (2400 Massachusetts Avenue, Cambridge, 617-547-2404) caters to the spending habits of babysitting and lawn-mowing moguls with — in addition to the usual higher priced items like stuffed animals, games, and crafts — rows of goldfish bowls filled with plastic dinosaurs, rubber eyeballs, and other necessities of the grade school set. In another nice twist, this small store has novelty items aimed at grown-ups, too. Note the Devil Duck — a satanic variation on the classic rubber ducky made for "very hot baths." There is also scented soap sold by the slice, jewelry, and candles.

SECRET
20TH-CENTURY ARTIFACTS

Collene is an antique brat. Her dad was an antiques dealer, and she caught the bug as an adult. She moved to Boston in her twenties and promised herself that before her 30th birthday, she'd have her own store. The result is **Absolutely Fabulous** (108 Beacon Street, Somerville, 617-864-0656), which Collene owns and operates along with partner Mara. Not only does Ab Fab have some of the best 20th-century treasures in town, but it's also one of those shops where people like to drop by to chat, or hang out on the gloopy blue kidney-shaped couch — when it isn't full of overflow merchandise. Look for vintage clothing, groovy barware, glittery encrusted sunglasses, painted furniture, and that endangered species: the Bakelite ashtray.

What Once Was (169 Brighton Avenue, Allston, 617-787-7898), for years an Inman Square staple, has moved to Allston, where it continues to stock vintage clothing, jewelry, and *objets d'art* "from deco to disco." In Lower Mills, **Streamline** (1162 Washington Avenue, 617-298-3326) has a nutty collection of almost-antique curios. Browse through vintage clothing from Don Ho Hawaiian shirts to Garbo-style chenille bathrobes. Bakelite jewelry shares shelf space with classic Sunbeam mixers, nut dishes, tiki cocktail glasses, and coconut brassieres. It's open Thursday to Sunday (noon to 5 PM). Get up a downmarket wedding party at **Oona's** (1210 Massachusetts Avenue, Cambridge, 617-491-2654). Among heaps of great old clothing, there are vintage wedding gowns from the 1940s to the 1980s. The groom can get his duds at **Keezer's** (140 River Street, 617-547-2455), one train stop away, where he'll find dozens of racks of used designer suits, as well as new and used tuxedoes for sale and for rent.

Selling vintage furniture from the '40s, '50s, and '60s, as well as retro-inspired items, **Abodeon** (1731 Massachusetts Avenue, Cambridge, 617-497-0137) is a cool time warp to those wacky decades. Look for kidney-shaped tables, starburst clocks, martini glasses, and a record room stocked with everything from cheap 45s to collectors' vinyl.

While Abodeon's wares are pricey, nearby **Dagmar's** (1702 Massachusetts Avenue, Cambridge, 617-758-0110) deals in slightly scuffed-up items of a similar vintage with a bit more of a kitsch quotient, as well as leather jackets and jeans. If you want to go upscale — think Herman Miller, Knoll, Dunbar — visit **Machine Age** (354 Congress Street, 617-482-0048), in South Boston. It's by far the largest — with its 13,000-square-foot showroom — and longest running of Boston's mod furniture stores, selling vintage and new furniture, sculpture, and retro knickknacks for more than a decade.

Finally, if bent steel and molded plastic hold no charm for you, remember that the late, great 20th century also produced the Mission style. Originating in the American West, this offshoot of the Arts and Crafts movement is showcased at **J. Austin Antiques** (1361 Cambridge Street, Cambridge, 617-234-4444), where durable Mission-style oak furniture, with its clean straight lines, decorates an intimate store.

ULTIMATE FRISBEE

Flick, hammer, scoober, blade, huck. Like any subculture, Ultimate Frisbee is full of jargon. (Tip: these are a few of the ways players can fling the disc.) A non-contact team sport played with a Frisbee (or disc) on a grass field with end zones, Ultimate moves like football, but its inner workings are more akin to basketball and soccer. Given its obscurity as an American sport, Ultimate doesn't often get mentioned in lists of Boston superlatives. Nevertheless, the **Boston Ultimate Disc Alliance** (BUDA, 617-484-1539) is the largest Ultimate Frisbee league in the United States. And its top teams — in both men's and women's divisions — are famous (in certain circles) for winning national championships. Many of these same Boston players are called up annually to compete with the US team against other countries.

BUDA players at all skill levels tend to thumb their noses at other area disc leagues as being strictly social. BUDA is also very social, but it prides itself on balancing that with doses of zealous competition. BUDA's social scene forms an entire lifestyle for some players, defining not only whom players hang out with, but also who does their accounting and whom they marry. As far as competition goes, teams vary widely, from Zen-like nonchalance to Kublai Khan ferocity. Players who persist will eventually find a comfortable level somewhere in the league (and, the good Lord willing, their future spouse).

There are several ways to get involved in Boston's gnarly Ultimate scene. Those who know the rules or can at least throw a Frisbee with some élan (even if they don't know what a huck is) are welcome at pick-up games. They happen all over, but the most reliable one takes place most Saturdays (1 PM to 3 PM) year round on the Charles River Esplanade between the Longfellow Bridge and the *Museum of Science*. The game goes on rain or shine, but always check the BUDA Web site (www.buda.org) for late updates.

Novices can sign up with one of the learning leagues, available in a variety of flavors (men's, women's, children's). To get a head start, look up "Ultimate in 10 Simple Rules" at the Ultimate Players Association Web site (www.upa.org/ultimate/rules/10simplerules.shtml).

Those who want to play with a team for a season join the "hat" league; these teams are created at random by the BUDA administration, so you don't have to know anyone to get in. Once players have shown their mettle in pick-ups or in hat leagues, they often jump into self-organized teams in the "open" leagues, which play together year after year. Finally, "club" Ultimate is for the top players, who may travel to compete in the Ultimate Players Association (UPA) national championships. To get on a club team, you usually have to attend a tryout. And you have to have an awesome scoober.

SECRET
UPPITY WOMEN

The Puritan Anne Hutchinson (1591–1643) figured God didn't play favorites. In her view, it was faith alone that paved the way to heaven (not how much money you could donate to the cause). Radically miffed at Hutchinson's unorthodox views, as well as her insistence on teaching them, the young colony's clergy banished Hutchinson from Massachusetts Bay. She went on to become one of the founders of Rhode Island, before being killed by Indians at the age of 43. Another woman, Mary Dyer, also stood up for religious freedom during the first years of the colony. Dyer, a Quaker, was hanged for heresy in 1660.

In the 1920s, statues were erected on the front west and east wings of Boston's *State House* to these two pioneers of religious freedom. Yet their stories and countless other narratives of the lives of Boston women are among the mightiest secrets of all those that the city harbors. Fortunately, a group of contemporary Boston women has taken a page from the Freedom Trail and the Black Heritage Trail to create the **Boston Women's Heritage Trail** (617-522-2872). Embracing four centuries of women's achievements, the BWHT is divided into five distinct walks: Downtown, the North End, Beacon Hill, South Cove/Chinatown, and the Back Bay. Unlike the Freedom Trail, where monuments and museums abound, many of the sites on the Women's Trail are evoked only in words. In some ways, this makes the trail all the more poignant, as visitors observe first hand how the physical reminders of women's history in Boston have been erased, but not altogether forgotten.

In addition to Hutchinson and Dyer, the trail visits several of the Freedom Trail's hallowed halls, putting a new spin on the story of how the nation was born. At the Old South Meeting House, we meet Phillis Wheatley, the first African-American poet to be published in book form; and the Paul Revere House becomes the Rachel and Paul Revere House, where Rachel kept the family business going while Paul ran the Revolution. The trail also visits the last Boston home of Louisa May Alcott, as well as the African Meeting House, which was a center for abolitionists and feminists like Maria Stewart and Julia Ward Howe. In the 20th century, the BWHT celebrates, among many others, the extraordinary lives of art collector Isabella Stewart Gardner and poet Anne Sexton, whose career as a poet began when she took a writing workshop at the Boston Center for Adult Education.

Guidebooks can be ordered from the Boston Women's Heritage Trail (above) or purchased at the **Boston National Park Service head-quarters** (15 State Street, 617-242-5642). In addition, the National Park Service offers women's history tours of the Freedom Trail. The Boston Park Rangers give "Women's Herstory Walks" on **Boston Common** (617-635-7383) on Sundays in May.

Named after the African-American feminist and abolitionist, Sojourner Truth, *Sojourner* (617-524-0415) is a monthly feminist newspaper covering national, regional, and local women's issues. There's a thick arts-and-events section and superb film reviews, and its ads are a parade of women-centered services and businesses. The community bulletin board lists local and national self-help resources. All that and a Marxist-feminist astrologer. Look for *Sojourner* and a profusion of other women's publications and resources at *New Words* (see "Secret Bookstores").

S E C R E T

USED MUSIC

Prowl any Boston commercial center, and you're likely to find at least one dim little shop selling pre-owned music in all its manifest forms, from dog-eared record albums that (who knows?) could be worth a fortune someday, all the way to CDs and DVDs, and even the occasional eight-track tape.

In a way, it's a neighborhood thing. You have your local used music shop; it's constantly freshening up its stock; you know the people who work there. There are, however, some places worth traveling out of your own orbit for. One of them is **Rhythm & Muse** (403A Centre Street, Jamaica Plain, 617-524-6622), a soulful place of exposed brick and wood frame that blends the selling of coffee, pastries, books, and CDs in a single cozy room. The music side features modern rock, blues, folk, and country, pausing in Boston for a look at the local music scene. There are listening stations where you can try out any of the used disks, as well as sample stations featuring selected new titles. But here's the amazing thing about R&M: for serious shoppers, they'll open new CDs to let you listen before you buy. "We feel it's important that people get something they know they're going to like," says the shopkeeper. What a concept. A happy byproduct of this enlightened policy is that the store sometimes has new CDs, unwrapped, that it sells for a 10-percent discount. R&M doesn't stock vinyl, but staffers are happy to take special orders.

For used vinyl, **Record Hog** (368 Beacon Street, Somerville, 617-868-HOGS) is a newcomer located in a wedge-shaped building on the Cambridge-Somerville line. Root through troughs of disks, mostly vintage vinyl (from Abba to ZZ Top), or check out the CDs, which are haphazardly lined up according to themes. The albums are the main event, with crates of them stacked everywhere. People even sit on them — the cats are usually hogging the barcaloungers. The store turns over a few hundred records each week, so many people make a habit of visiting on a regular basis.

Disk Diggers (401 Highland Avenue, 617-776-7560) has the amazing wall of eight-tracks, which may be reason enough to visit this Davis Square mainstay. Music here tends toward the esoteric. Rock is most prevalent, but there's also a decent selection of world music, jazz, and blues.

The granddaddy of Greater Boston's used music stores, **Cheapo Records** (645 Massachusetts Avenue, Cambridge, 617-354-4455), is still kicking in Central Square despite the domino effect of recent large-scale gentrification there. Blues, jazz, and world music are the stock-in-trade of this basement shop.

These stores post flyers for local bands and distribute most of the area music 'zines, so they're good places to find out who's playing around town.

S E C R E T
USEFUL THINGS

You know those ecru coffee mugs favored by greasy spoon restaurants? You know those plastic ketchup and mustard squeeze bottles? How about those cafeteria-style fiberglass trays in crayon colors that you used to put your plate of spaghetti-Os on in elementary school? All that is just the beginning of what you can find at **Harbour Food Service Equipment** (119 North Washington Street, 617-227-8300), a restaurant equipment store on the brink of Boston's North End. Some of the items here seem to be purely for show: whisks the size of major-league baseball bats, Big Dipper-sized ladles (well, almost). And ashtrays! Who uses these things? Other products are clearly aimed at the professional, like the 12-burner stainless steel ovens and starched chef's hats. In the basement, shelves are loaded with half-price Fiestaware and "greenline" diner china vying with odds and ends too numerous to catalog. A few doors down from Harbour is **Eastern Baker's Supply** (145 North Washington Street, 617-742-0228), offering pretty much the same set of wares but with an added veneer of dust. You just can't help feeling you're going to find a whopping bargain here as you wander the cramped aisles, hopeless of assistance from the absentee clerks.

In the heart of the North End, **Salem Street Hardware** (89 Salem Street, 617-523-4759) may look like a run-of-the-mill hammer and nail shop, but inside you'll find everything you need to equip your own Italian kitchen. While the store does stock plenty of hardware, it's stuffed to the rafters, in an organized fashion, with pasta makers, pizza stones, pasta bowls, and the like. In a similar vein, Chinatown's **Food Service Equipment & Supply** (Chauncy Street, no telephone number available) has everything you need to make fried rice for multitudes: woks the size of truck tires, industrial rice steamers, and plenty of handy and astoundingly cheap items for small-time cooks as well.

At the **Museum of Useful Things** (370 Broadway, Cambridge, 617-576-3322), a Cambridge household gadget store, I looked lovingly on chunky-handled oxo kitchen utensils, spring-loaded metal napkin holders, and 1950s-style tins of garden twine that allow you unroll and snip without the tangle. But what got me was the "Boston" brand metal and rubber vacuum-mounted pencil sharpener. If I had one of these, I surmised, think of the hooky I could play from my writing desk. Useful? You bet. I also liked the idea of having my morning java in a lab beaker, as suggested by the store's 250- or 350-milliliter size mugs. Fully caffeinated, I'd grab my brushed aluminum lunch box (made in China), and off to the factory with me. This place could be a prop shop for Jacques Tati.

Salad spinners, doormats, pepper mills, dish towels, rolling pins, and stacks of dishes and drinking glasses: there's rarely anything remarkable at **China Fair** (2100 Massachusetts Avenue, Cambridge, 617-864-3050). But this no-nonsense kitchenware emporium, up north on Mass Ave, has basic prices on the basics, making it the place to check first. If, however, it's style you're after, move on to **Bliss** (2257 Massachusetts Avenue, Cambridge, 888-325-BLISS), where European and American designers call the shots. This is primarily a bridal registry, but why should brides have all the fun? The tiny store is expertly laid out with displays of unusual gifts, fine china (Alessi, Calvin Klein, Sasaki, Wedgwood), flatware, and crystal, as well as a few furniture pieces of post-mod steel and molded plastic.

In the South End, **Laboratory** (577 Tremont Street, 617-266-7300) urges "home experimentation," stocking Alvar Aalto free-form vases,

indoor-outdoor furniture like the "Oh" chair ($40), and "paper clip" bookshelves, as well as desk accessories and gifts. And **Fresh Eggs** (58 Clarendon Street, 617-247-8150) dazzles with stylish kitchen implements, bathroom fashion statements, and silk robes. I especially like the hand-blown glass hanging lamps in vibrant colors.

S E C R E T
VEGETARIAN

While many Boston restaurants devote a portion of their menu to non-carnivores, there are few strictly vegetarian places in this meat-and-potatoes town. A happy exception is **Masao's Kitchen** (581 Moody Street, Waltham, 781-647-7977), a casual macrobiotic restaurant in downtown Waltham. Masao's list of "no's" is reassuring to those who care greatly about what they eat: no refined sugar, no MSG, no preservatives or irradiation, no tropical oils or genetically engineered foods. On the other hand, the cooking and the atmosphere are decidedly positive. Pick a table at this sunny storefront, then sidle up to the buffet ($9.50) to fill your plate with udon noodles sautéed with tofu, carrots, onion, greens, and ginger; adzuki beans and squash; rich lentil stew; and hearty vegetables. Or go for a freshly made sandwich: tofu burgers, veggie burgers, tempeh, or seitan cutlets are served on big slices of chewy sourdough bread with soy-based mayonnaise and ribbons of sliced red onion. There's sushi, too. For dessert, a slice of warm cherry or apple cake awaits. For drinks, there are bottled iced teas and juices, barley tea, and black teas. If you like, you can bring in your own containers for take-out. Open Monday to Wednesday (noon to 8 PM), and Thursday to Saturday (noon to 9 PM).

Fake meats made from seitan (for chicken and beef), tofu (for pork), and root vegetables (for seafood) are the curious staples at the vegan, Asian restaurant **Grasshopper** (1 North Beacon Street, 617-254-8883). To get the full spectrum, go for the house special of vermicelli rice noodles. It comes with an array of fake meats, including a convincing chunk of pork, which turns out to be toast. It's not going to fool anyone, but it tastes great. Also recommended: the Vietnamese pizza appetizer. While Grasshopper's ambiance is almost elegant — with nice touches like pebbles to rest your chopsticks on — one could eat lunch (11 AM to 3 PM) very cheaply here by sticking to the specials. Imagine a lunch of stir-fried mixed vegetables with tofu and a spring roll, along with the soup of the day, steamed or fried rice, and jasmine tea — all for under $5.

Davis Square has a couple of places that rarely get cited in veggie circles, but should. **Celia's** (236 Elm Street, Somerville, 617-591-1922) has a complete array of gourmet vegan prepared dishes, sandwiches, and soups. And **Diesel Café** (257 Elm Street, Somerville, 617-629-8717) does tasty vegan cookies.

SECRET

WEATHER

Do the words "wintry mix" mean anything to you? Spend a few days in Boston between November and April, and they will. It's a weathercaster's euphemism for what passes for snow in Boston: freezing rain mixed with big wet flakes, sleet, hail, and various doodads from the sky. Another thing visitors and newcomers to Boston notice: umbrellas are useless here because it rains sideways. Also, spring only comes once in a decade. So, despite being at the same latitude as Rome, Boston's climate is a far cry from *la dolce vita.* Boston weather, I'm told, arrives from the West, producing hot summers and cold winters. Our oceanside location adds special effects like slushy springtimes, autumn hurricanes, and North Atlantic winter storms called "northeasters" for their wind direction.

Still, all you really need to know about Boston weather is the little ditty that explains how to read the **weather lights** atop the old Hancock Tower in the Back Bay. It goes something like this: "Steady blue, clear view. Flashing blue, clouds due. Steady red, rain ahead. Flashing red, snow instead." (However, during baseball season, flashing red means the Sox game has been called off.)

Like a miniature castle in a miniature mountain aerie, the **Blue Hills Observatory Weather Museum and Science Center** (near Canton Avenue, Route 138, and Observatory Access Road, Milton, 617-696-1014) stands atop not-so-very-lofty Great Blue Hill in Milton. Founded in 1885 as a private scientific station for the study of weather and the atmosphere, over the years this station has been the site of a number of heady scientific inquiries on clouds, rainfall patterns, and radiation. Plans are afoot for the observatory to set up a museum of meteorology in the near future. For now, the observatory is open weekends (except in deep winter), with tours offered from 11 AM to 3 PM; $2.

S E C R E T
YOGA

Boston has a first-rate yoga culture, with internationally respected teachers in many branches of this 2,000-year-old art. First stop is a rubber yoga mat at **Baron Baptiste Power Yoga Institute** (2000 Massachusetts Avenue, Cambridge, 617-661-YOGA). Five times a day at this Cambridge studio, 60 bodies cram into a room that's heated to 90 degrees for an hour and a half of what Baptiste calls "sweat and spirituality." In fact, while cups runneth over with perspiration, these classes are social occasions — a better place for a hot date than for finding God. Still, I know of no better workout. Classes, which are cheap ($10) compared to those at other area yoga schools, are taught by Baptiste and his disciples. To find out who's teaching and when, call the hotline (above).

Baptiste's own former guru is the Hollywood yogi Bikram Choudhury, whose disciples have opened a studio in downtown Boston. **Bikram Yoga** (108 Lincoln Street, 617-556-9926) classes are reportedly hotter and harder than Baptiste's.

At Barbara Benagh's **Yoga Studio** (74 Joy Street, 617-523-7138), you can also do vinyasa — or "flow"-style — yoga, as well as Iyengar-style yoga, which focuses on strength rather than stamina. The studio also offers instruction in meditation, and classes for breast cancer survivors and asthmatics. Benagh has been teaching yoga on Beacon Hill since 1980. The matriarch of Iyengar yoga in Boston, however, is Patricia Walden of yoga video and *Time* magazine fame. Her **BKS Iyengar Yoga Center of Greater Boston** (240A Elm Street, Somerville, 617-666-9551) is located in Davis Square. The focus is on precise alignment in the postures and on the use of props to allow even non-Gumbies to get a delicious stretch. The center's 12 teachers offer classes every day of the week for all levels.

SECRET FUTURE

It was little old me who wrote this book. No ad hoc committees, no focus groups. *Secret Boston* reflects what I found, what captured my interest, and what I thought worth passing along. That said, I probably missed something essential — some out-of-sight sight, some hidden hoard, some pocket park, wacky event, or arcane artistic venue. And, frankly, you're aghast.

Well, native Bostonian Ben Franklin put it best: "I should have no objection to go over the same life from its beginning to the end: requesting only the advantage authors have, of correcting in a second edition the faults of the first."

In other words, not to worry. If you know of a place that deserves inclusion in future editions of *Secret Boston,* just let us know. If we use your suggestion, we'll send you a free copy on publication. Please contact us at the following address:

Secret Boston
c/o ECW PRESS

2120 Queen Street East, Suite 200
Toronto, Ontario, Canada M4E 1E2

Or e-mail us at: info@secretguides.com

PHOTO SITES

SUBJECT INDEX

SECRET BOSTON

Child's Play

Coffee/Tea/Other Non-Alcoholic Beverages

Ethnic Eateries

ALPHABETICAL INDEX